Microsoft 365 Mobili

Security – Exam Guide MS-101

Explore threat management, governance, security, compliance, and device services in Microsoft 365

Nate Chamberlain

BIRMINGHAM - MUMBAI

Microsoft 365 Mobility and Security – Exam Guide MS-101

Copyright © 2019 Packt Publishing

Commissioning Editor: Vijin Boricha
Acquisition Editor: Rohit Rajkumar
Content Development Editor: Ronn Kurien
Senior Editor: Richard Brookes-Bland
Technical Editor: Prachi Sawant
Copy Editor: Safis Editing
Project Coordinator: Anish Daniel
Proofreader: Safis Editing
Indexer: Priyanka Dhadke
Production Designer: Nilesh Mohite

First published: November 2019

Production reference: 1281119

Published by Packt Publishing Ltd.
Livery Place
35 Livery Street
Birmingham
B3 2PB, UK.

ISBN 978-1-83898-465-6

www.packt.com

To my husband and best friend, William Ottens. I love you.
Our adventures have only just begun.

Packt.com

Subscribe to our online digital library for full access to over 7,000 books and videos, as well as industry leading tools to help you plan your personal development and advance your career. For more information, please visit our website.

Why subscribe?

- Spend less time learning and more time coding with practical eBooks and Videos from over 4,000 industry professionals

- Improve your learning with Skill Plans built especially for you

- Get a free eBook or video every month

- Fully searchable for easy access to vital information

- Copy and paste, print, and bookmark content

Did you know that Packt offers eBook versions of every book published, with PDF and ePub files available? You can upgrade to the eBook version at www.packt.com and as a print book customer, you are entitled to a discount on the eBook copy. Get in touch with us at customercare@packtpub.com for more details.

At www.packt.com, you can also read a collection of free technical articles, sign up for a range of free newsletters, and receive exclusive discounts and offers on Packt books and eBooks.

Contributors

About the author

Nate Chamberlain is a Microsoft MVP in Office apps and services from Lawrence, Kansas, where he also created and leads the Lawrence SharePoint User Group (LSPUG). Nate's experience in the education and healthcare industries has contributed to his diverse skill set and knowledge around change management, technology integration, systems administration, end user adoption and governance, and training development and execution. He has a master's degree in library and information science, a bachelor's degree in business administration, and is an M365 Certified Enterprise Administrator Expert. Nate also published *The ABCs of SharePoint* and *Rise of the Advocates* and has written over 200 blog posts at NateChamberlain.com.

Thank you to all of my community connections who have offered their knowledge, experience, support, and friendship. And, most of all, I want to thank my husband William for his unfailing love and support.

About the reviewer

Peter Daalmans is a principal consultant and trainer at Daalmans Consulting with a primary focus on Microsoft System Center Configuration Manager and Enterprise Mobility. Peter has been awarded a Microsoft Enterprise Mobility MVP every year since 2012.

He writes blog posts and shares his knowledge on his blog, `ConfigMgrBlog.com`. He is the author of books such as *Mastering System Center 2012 Configuration Manager, Mastering System Center 2012 R2 Configuration Manager, Mastering System Center Configuration Manager (Current Branch)*, and *Microsoft Enterprise Mobility Suite: Planning and Implementation*.

He speaks at conferences such as Microsoft Ignite, Microsoft TechEd, IT/Dev Connections, TechMentor, Techorama, Midwest Management Summit, BriForum, TechDays, and ExpertsLive.

Packt is searching for authors like you

If you're interested in becoming an author for Packt, please visit `authors.packtpub.com` and apply today. We have worked with thousands of developers and tech professionals, just like you, to help them share their insight with the global tech community. You can make a general application, apply for a specific hot topic that we are recruiting an author for, or submit your own idea.

Table of Contents

Section 3: Microsoft 365 Governance Compliance

Preface

Thank you for buying *Microsoft 365 Mobility and Security – Exam Guide MS 101*. This book will help you prepare for the MS-101 exam by understanding the *Skills measured*, which are mentioned on the exam's official page, and testing your knowledge with practice questions. While I will cover every topic listed for the exam, I cannot include every question, as they are known only to the exam administrators to help protect the integrity of the exam.

Who this book is for

The target audience for this exam guide is anyone aspiring to take the MS-101 exam to validate their competency in Microsoft 365 Enterprise Mobility and Security.

If you're taking the MS-101 exam, then chances are you may also be pursuing a certification and, in particular, the Microsoft 365 Enterprise Administrator Expert certification. You can refer to *The exam* and *Certification* sections for more information.

What this book covers

This book covers every exam objective outlined in the MS-101 exam's documentation. Each chapter represents an exam objective, divided among three parts, representing the skills measured in the exam:

Section 1, *Modern Device Services (30-35% of the exam)*:

Chapter 1, *Implementing Mobile Device Management (MDM)*, introduces you to planning for **mobile device management** (**MDM**), configuring MDM integration with Azure AD, setting an MDM authority, and setting the device enrollment limit for users.

Chapter 2, *Managing Device Compliance*, explores how to plan for device compliance; configure device compliance policies; and design, create, and manage conditional access policies.

Chapter 3, *Planning for Devices and Apps*, teaches you how to prepare your organization's Microsoft Store for Business, plan app deployment, device comanagement, device monitoring, device profiles, **mobile application management** (**MAM**), and mobile device security.

Chapter 4, *Planning Windows 10 Deployment*, looks at planning for **Windows as a Service (WaaS)**, planning your Windows 10 deployment method, analyzing Windows 10 upgrade readiness, and evaluating and deploying Windows 10 security features.

Section 2, *Microsoft 365 Security and Threat Management (30-35% of the exam)*:

Chapter 5, *Implementing Cloud App Security (CAS)*, looks at designing and configuring **Cloud App Security (CAS)** and its policies, configuring connected apps, managing CAS alerts, and uploading CAS traffic logs.

Chapter 6, *Implementing Threat Management*, shows you how to plan a threat management solution, design and configure Azure **Advanced Threat Protection (ATP)** and Microsoft 365 ATP policies, and monitor **Advanced Threat Analytics (ATA)** incidents.

Chapter 7, *Implementing Windows Defender ATP*, shows you how to plan your Windows Defender ATP solution, configure preferences, implement policies, and enable security features of Windows 10.

Chapter 8, *Managing Security Reports and Alerts*, shows you how to manage the service assurance dashboard, use tracing and reporting on Azure AD Identity Protection, and configure and manage Microsoft 365 and Azure Identity Protection alerts.

Section 3, *Microsoft 365 Governance and Compliance (35-40% of the exam)*:

Chapter 9, *Configuring Data Loss Prevention (DLP)*, explores how to design and configure **data loss prevention (DLP)** policies, manage DLP exceptions, and monitor and manage DLP policy matches.

Chapter 10, *Implementing Azure Information Protection (AIP)*, teaches you how to plan your **Azure Information Protection (AIP)** solution, deploy the on-premises rights management connector, plan for **Windows Information Protection (WIP)** and classification labeling, configure **Information Rights Management (IRM)** for workloads, configure the superuser, deploy AIP clients, implement AIP policies, and implement your AIP tenant key.

Chapter 11, *Managing Data Governance*, shows you how to configure information retention, plan for Microsoft 365 backups, restore deleted content, and plan information retention policies.

Chapter 12, *Managing Auditing*, teaches you how to configure audit log retention, your audit policy, and monitor unified audit logs.

Chapter 13, *Managing eDiscovery*, enables you to search for content using the Security and Compliance center, plan for in-place and legal holds, and configure e-Discovery.

Section 4, *Mock Exams*

Chapter 14, *Mock Exam 1*, contains 20 questions to help you prepare for the exam.

Chapter 15, *Mock Exam 2*, contains another 20 questions to further help you prepare for taking MS-101.

Book structure

If I were using this book, I would do the following:

1. Start with the **mock exams** and **chapter reviews** (noting your answers on a separate piece of paper or an electronic device).
2. Check your answers against the *Assessment* section.
3. If you miss something, check out the relevant chapters and support articles and freshen up. If you get a question right, you may not need to spend so much time on that topic.
4. Plan your studying based on your weaknesses or areas in which you're less familiar.

But everybody learns differently and you may best benefit from working through the book, front to back. In that case, here's how the book is organized:

- There is one chapter per skill measured, and each subtopic is covered in a section within that chapter.
- Each chapter ends with a *Questions* (with two practice questions) section and a *Further reading* section with links to the relevant documentation. I'd recommend checking out the documentation for any topic you're uncertain about.
- There are two *mock exams* at the end of the book, with an *Assessments* chapter at the very end with answers to all chapter reviews and the two exams. Each question's answer is supported with an explanation and a link to more information (this is more up to date than print can be, so check when needed).

This book assumes a general familiarity with Microsoft 365 apps and services, such as SharePoint and Azure Active Directory. Taking the MS-100: Microsoft 365 Identity and Services exam *first* is advisable, and will help make sure you have a foundational knowledge of some of the core Microsoft 365 concepts you'll lean on in the MS-101 exam.

The exam

The exam's official web page is https://www.microsoft.com/en-us/learning/exam-ms-101.aspx. I always recommend checking the exam information page to make sure you're preparing for the latest skills included. Things in the Microsoft world change quickly, and new concepts may be added at any time.

The exam page allows you to schedule your exam (to take it remotely at your home or at a certified test center) and review the skills measured in the exam. Currently, it lists the following:

- Implement modern device services (30-35%)
- Implement Microsoft 365 security and threat management (30-35%)
- Manage Microsoft 365 governance and compliance (35-40%)

You'll notice these match the three parts to this book outlined in the *Table of Contents*. Within each of the three parts, the book is broken into chapters in which you'll find the specific skills measured and their associated subtopics.

Certification

I wrote this book after having successfully taken and passed the exam myself, and now I have the **Microsoft 365 Certified: Enterprise Administrator Expert** certification.

The Microsoft 365 Enterprise Administrator Expert certification is obtained through accomplishing the following steps:

1. Obtain **one** (1) of these five (5) certifications:
   - Teamwork Administrator (MS-300 + MS-301)
   - Modern Desktop Administrator Associate (MD-100 + MD-101)
   - Security Administrator Associate (MS-500)
   - Messaging Administrator Associate (MS-200 + MS-201, or Transition Exam MS-202)
   - MCSE Productivity (refer to https://www.microsoft.com/en-us/learning/mcse-productivity-certification.aspx)
2. **Pass MS-100**: Microsoft 365 Identity and Services
3. **Pass MS-101**: Microsoft 365 Mobility and Security

How to get the most out of this book

While this book alone will introduce you to concepts and refresh your memory on topics you may be less familiar with, you can maximize your studies by practicing and exploring what you're learning first-hand in an actual tenant.

As you'll find in this book, it's recommended that you get a Microsoft 365 E5 subscription in order to explore, but you could also combine a Microsoft 365 E3 trial with an Enterprise Mobility and Security E5 trial to cover most of the book's topics. In the end, what matters most is that you make sure you get a trial or a subscription to the services and apps you feel least confident with so that you can spend time exploring them first hand.

Download the color images

We also provide a PDF file that has color images of the screenshots/diagrams used in this book. You can download it here: `https://static.packt-cdn.com/downloads/9781838984656_ColorImages.pdf`.

Conventions used

There are a number of text conventions used throughout this book.

`CodeInText`: Indicates code words in text, database table names, folder names, filenames, file extensions, pathnames, dummy URLs, user input, and Twitter handles. Here is an example: "Mount the downloaded `WebStorm-10*.dmg` disk image file as another disk in your system."

Any command-line input or output is written as follows:

```
Set-Mailbox 'Nate Chamberlain' -AuditEnabled $true
```

Bold: Indicates a new term, an important word, or words that you see on screen. For example, words in menus or dialog boxes appear in the text like this. Here is an example: "Click on **Site Collection Audit Settings** under **Site Collection Administration**."

Warnings or important notes appear like this.

Tips and tricks appear like this.

Get in touch

Feedback from our readers is always welcome.

General feedback: If you have questions about any aspect of this book, mention the book title in the subject of your message and email us at customercare@packtpub.com.

Errata: Although we have taken every care to ensure the accuracy of our content, mistakes do happen. If you have found a mistake in this book, we would be grateful if you would report this to us. Please visit www.packtpub.com/support/errata, selecting your book, clicking on the Errata Submission Form link, and entering the details.

Piracy: If you come across any illegal copies of our works in any form on the internet, we would be grateful if you would provide us with the location address or website name. Please contact us at copyright@packt.com with a link to the material.

If you are interested in becoming an author: If there is a topic that you have expertise in and you are interested in either writing or contributing to a book, please visit authors.packtpub.com.

Reviews

Please leave a review. Once you have read and used this book, why not leave a review on the site that you purchased it from? Potential readers can then see and use your unbiased opinion to make purchase decisions, we at Packt can understand what you think about our products, and our authors can see your feedback on their book. Thank you!

For more information about Packt, please visit packt.com.

Section 1: Modern Device Services

In this section, we will focus on implementing modern device services, which makes up 30-35% of the MS-101 exam. Here, you'll learn how to utilize the services and settings you can control as a Microsoft 365 modern device administrator.

This section includes the following chapters:

- Chapter 1, *Implementing Mobile Device Management (MDM)*
- Chapter 2, *Managing Device Compliance*
- Chapter 3, *Planning for Devices and Apps*
- Chapter 4, *Planning Windows 10 Deployment*

1
Implementing Mobile Device Management (MDM)

Mobile Device Management (**MDM**) allows you to take your organization's security, compliance requirements, and configuring your enterprise MDM settings to match so that devices accessing company resources and data are monitored and secure. MDM helps you to control who and under which circumstances users can access company data, minimizing the likelihood of data loss or unauthorized access. While there are many third-party solutions for MDM, we'll focus primarily on the Microsoft solution, Intune.

In this chapter, we'll cover the following topics, including the basics of MDM planning:

- Planning for MDM
- Configuring MDM integration with Azure AD
- Setting an MDM authority
- Setting device enrollment limits for users

Planning for MDM

When thinking of your organization's path to MDM, you'll want to consider and assess your company's unique requirements. The exam will likely focus more on the settings and configuration of MDM, so we'll focus primarily on them. When you're ready to begin implementing MDM, you can generally break it down into the following 10 steps:

1. Configure the security groups in **Active Directory** (**AD**) or Azure AD that will allow you to easily assign policies or apply restrictions based on membership. Many of the later steps will depend on you thoughtfully creating these groups on which you'll base restrictions and permissions:

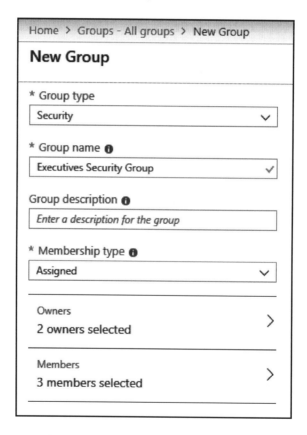

2. Assign Intune and Office 365 licenses to users from within the Microsoft 365 admin center (`admin.microsoft.com`) or Azure Active Directory. Users *must* be assigned an Intune license to be able to enroll their device.

3. Set your MDM authority to Intune (see the *Setting an MDM authority* section), and create an MDM push certificate for Apple devices (see the *Device types and enrollment* section).

4. Create terms and conditions via Intune | **Tenant Administration** | **Terms and Conditions** | **Create**, as seen in the following screenshot:

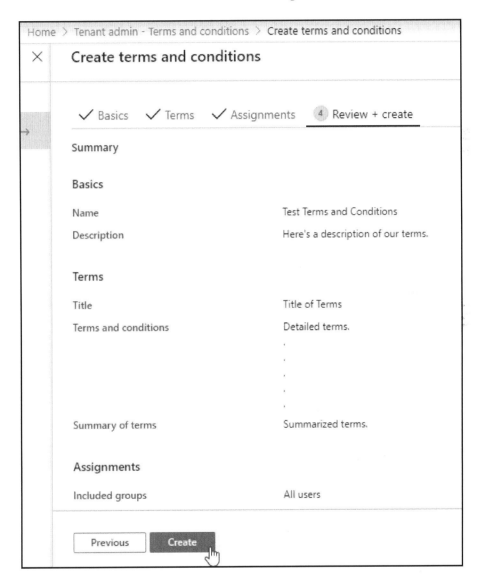

Deploying terms and conditions is optional, but requires users to accept your company's terms of usage prior to enrolling via the company portal. This can also be configured during setup of conditional access, which we'll discuss more in `Chapter 2`, *Managing Device Compliance:*

5. Deploy general/custom configuration policies (restrictions or allowances based on device types and groups). The following example of a configuration profile will block access to **Game Center** for iOS devices:

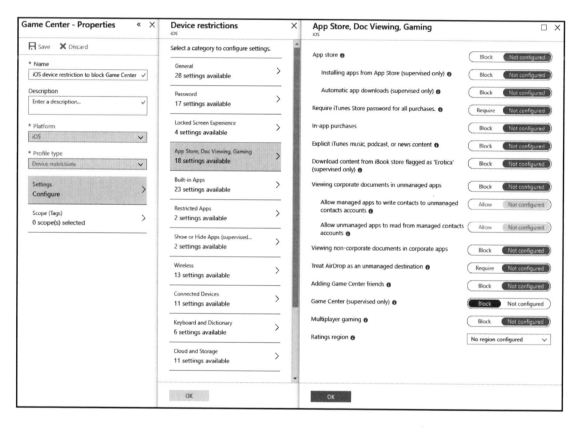

6. Deploy resource profiles (Wi-Fi, email, and VPN resources that can be deployed).
7. Deploy store or custom/line-of-business apps.
8. Deploy compliance policies to make sure users are using approved devices (specific OS versions, not jailbroken devices, and so on). The following example policy ensures iOS devices use passwords to unlock the device with at least four characters:

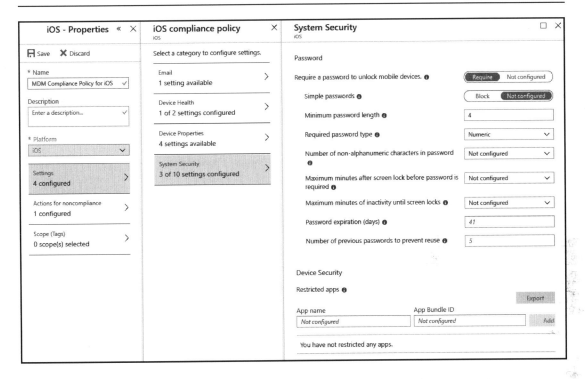

9. Enable conditional access policies that will restrict users from accessing company data if certain criteria aren't met, such as the compliance policies in *step 8*.
10. Finally, enroll the devices.

Next, we will look at device types.

Device types and enrollment

MDM-enrolled devices may be completely controlled by the company (such as those running Android Enterprise dedicated or iOS supervised modes) or could be **bring your own device** (**BYOD**), such as those running the Android Enterprise work profile where users enroll personal devices to access company resources but are left with the freedom to use their device normally outside of work apps and data.

Android Enterprise modes include the following:

- **Work profile**: Personal data is kept separate from corporate data.
- **Dedicated**: Meant for single-use devices where most links/apps are blocked.
- **Fully managed**: Corporate-owned devices fully managed by the company and intended for work only (not personal usage).

Android Device Administrator (or legacy) has been deprecated and is not encouraged since the Android Enterprise options are now available.

Furthermore, **iOS supervised** mode is essentially a checkbox you can mark for iOS devices during configuration in order to restrict functionality, such as renaming the device, AirPrint, AirDrop, and more. View a complete list of settings you can restrict in supervised mode at `https://docs.microsoft.com/en-us/intune/configuration/device-restrictions-ios`.

Windows and Android devices are supported by default, whereas iOS and macOS devices require setting up an **Apple push certificate** in the Intune/Microsoft 365 device management portal. If bulk enrolling via Apple Configurator, you'll also need to create the profile to be used. The following screenshot shows the **Device enrollment | Apple enrollment** screen of Intune, where you'll find the **Apple MDM Push certificate** setup option:

Intune requires an Apple MDM Push certificate to manage Apple devices, and supports multiple enrollment methods. Set up the MDM push certificate to begin. Learn More.

Prerequisites

Apple MDM Push certificate
Certificate required to manage Apple devices

Bulk enrollment methods

Apple Configurator
Manage Apple Configurator enrollment

Enrollment program tokens
Manage Device Enrollment Program and Apple School Manager

The Apple push certificate allows you to manage iOS and macOS devices in Intune. It must be renewed regularly, and it grants Microsoft permission to send user and device data to Apple.

Once the prerequisites are met, and you've obtained the Apple push certificate if needed, you can bulk enroll users or allow self-enrollment via the Company Portal app. Apple also has Apple Configurator, Apple School Manager, and Device Enrollment Program available as bulk enrollment methods.

Because Android devices, as an example, are supported by default, a user simply needs to self-enroll. To do so, follow these steps:

1. Install the Intune Company Portal app from Google Play.
2. Sign in with a work or school account.
3. Work through the prompts, choosing what the app is and isn't allowed to access. At some point, you will choose **BEGIN**:

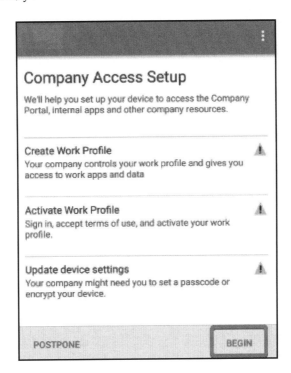

4. Depending on the settings configured by administrators, you may be prompted to update your passcode to meet the minimum security requirements before the device can complete enrollment and access company resources:

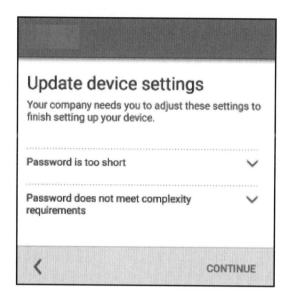

5. Once the required changes have been made to ensure the security of the device and the identity of the user accessing company data, the wizard will be complete. Click **Done** and then you can access resources and apps from the work profile.

You can learn more about enrolling specific devices at the following links:

- **Windows devices**: https://docs.microsoft.com/en-us/intune/windows-enrollment-methods
- **Android devices**: https://docs.microsoft.com/en-us/intune/android-enroll
- **iOS devices**: https://docs.microsoft.com/en-us/intune/ios-enroll
- **macOS devices**: https://docs.microsoft.com/en-us/intune/macos-enroll

In this section, we made a plan for setting up MDM and took a general look at the types of devices that can be enrolled in MDM. In the next section, we'll configure MDM using Azure AD.

Configuring MDM integration with Azure AD

The Azure AD mobility settings allow you, as an IT administrator, the ability to help ensure users are accessing company data and assets in a secure and compliant way, which you specify through configuring MDM integration within Azure AD. If your users are using personal or managed devices to access corporate data and apps, you'll want to configure MDM with Azure AD.

Registered versus joined devices

Azure AD **registered devices** are typically the personal devices in a BYOD scenario on which a user enters their work or school credentials to access their organization resources and data from an organization's domain. The previously mentioned Android and iOS enrollments would be registered devices.

For example, you might sign into your *personal* computer while connected to your *organization's* Wi-Fi and you need access to Active Directory for emailing and room reservations.

Azure AD **joined devices** are work owned, such as your work-issued laptop, and allow for easy deployment of Windows and features such as **Single Sign-On** (**SSO**), which don't require a user to be connected to an organization's domain to sign in.

If you already have devices joined to your on-premises Active Directory, you can configure a **hybrid Azure AD join** setup as well. This allows you to still benefit from any existing **group policy** (**GP**) configurations.

> You can learn more about planning MDM integration with Azure AD here:
>
> - **Azure AD join**: https://docs.microsoft.com/en-us/azure/active-directory/devices/azureadjoin-plan
> - **Hybrid Azure AD join**: https://docs.microsoft.com/en-us/azure/active-directory/devices/hybrid-azuread-join-plan

By default, your Azure AD **Device settings** allow users to join their devices to Azure AD. You can configure this as follows:

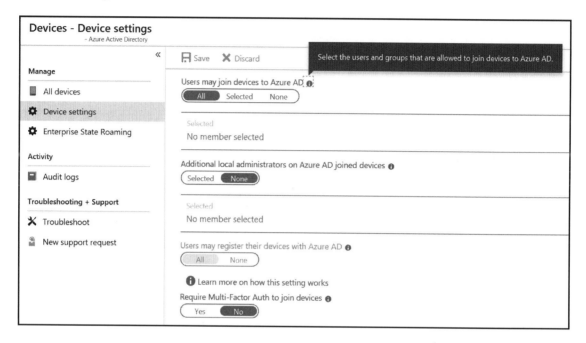

Next, we will set up automatic enrollment.

Setting up automatic enrollment

Setting up automatic enrollment requires **Microsoft Enterprise Mobility + Security (EMS)**/Azure Active Directory Premium. If you don't have this subscription but would like to follow along with the steps in this section, you will be prompted to start a trial when it is required for additional access and functionality. If you have the subscription, or opt to start the trial when prompted, be sure to assign a license to yourself before proceeding.

 Throughout this book, when discussing licensing, keep in mind you can use Azure AD to manage product licensing in groups rather than for each individual. When you add a member to the group, they're assigned the relevant licenses until they're removed from the group. Learn more at https://docs.microsoft.com/en-us/azure/active-directory/fundamentals/active-directory-licensing-whatis-azure-portal.

Assigning policies, permissions, licenses, and features like automatic enrollment for **All Users** is rarely appropriate. You'll want to be sure to use groups in Azure AD to make managing configurations over time easier and avoid changing the configuration itself as opposed to just managing group memberships.

In this section, we looked at the Azure AD role in MDM, discovered the differences between registered and joined devices, and set up automatic enrollment capabilities. Next, we will see how to select and set an MDM authority.

Setting an MDM authority

Setting an MDM authority gives your administrators the ability to manage the configuration settings for devices throughout your organization. Possible authorities include the following:

- Intune Standalone (configured in Azure)
- Intune co-management (configure using the System Center Configuration Manager console)
- Office 365 MDM (selected in the Microsoft 365 admin center)

When viewing the Intune/Microsoft 365 device management portal, you may see an orange banner prompting you to select an authority. If not, select an option such as **Device enrollment** to get the authority selection prompt:

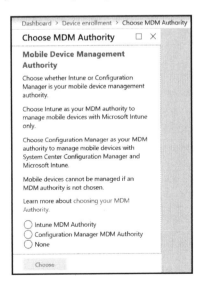

In this section, we selected an MDM authority. Now we'll set the device enrollment type and quantity limits.

Setting device enrollment limits for users

Device type restrictions in your MDM solution help make sure your organization is secure and compliant. This is achieved by ensuring devices used to access company data are running a supported platform (iOS, Android, and so on.) within specific version ranges and/or are corporate-owned versus personal devices. **Device limit restrictions** help your organization work within its available license structure, avoiding *over-licensing* any one individual and potentially running up costs to license the rest.

In the Intune portal under **Device enrollment** | **Enrollment restrictions,** you're able to create these restrictions and adjust their priority. Once you create a restriction, you then assign it to everyone or to specific user groups. These restrictions show up listed on the **Enrollment restrictions** view where you can select one to edit it or change its priority. When policies conflict, the highest priority policy applies:

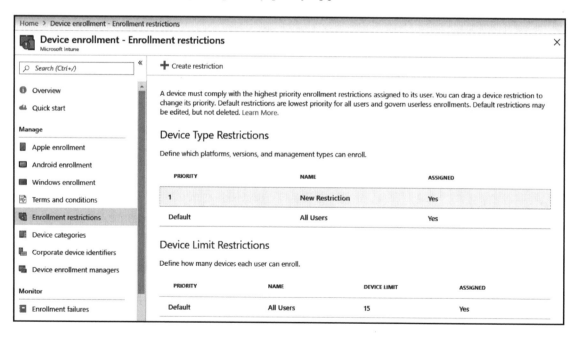

Now, let's look at device type restrictions.

Device type restrictions

When configuring device type restrictions, you choose prerequisites for devices connecting to company data. You're able to restrict devices based on their platform or the platform configuration. The following are restriction options available to you:

- Platforms (allow or block):
    - Android
    - Android Enterprise
    - iOS/iPadOS
    - macOS
    - Windows Phone 8.1
    - Windows 8.1 and later
    - Windows 10 and later

- Platform configurations:
    - Minimum version
    - Maximum version
    - Allow/block personally owned devices

Let's go ahead and create restrictions:

1. To create a restriction, go to **Azure** | **Device enrollment** | **Enrollment restrictions** and click **Create restriction**.
2. Select **Device type restriction** for the restriction type:

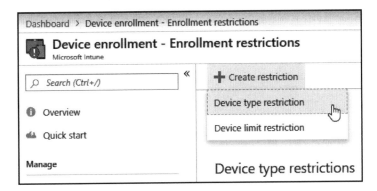

3. Name and describe your restriction. Click **Next**:

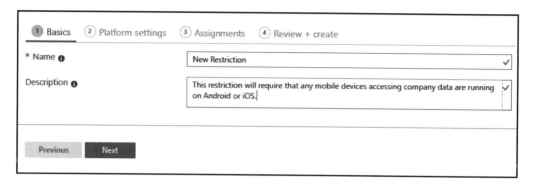

4. Because we selected **Device type restriction**, we must now configure the platform settings.
5. To allow access for a specific platform type, just toggle the **Allow/Block** switch. You can also *configure the minimum and maximum allowed versions* of each with the exception of macOS. The far-right toggle allows you to block personally owned devices of each platform type as well:

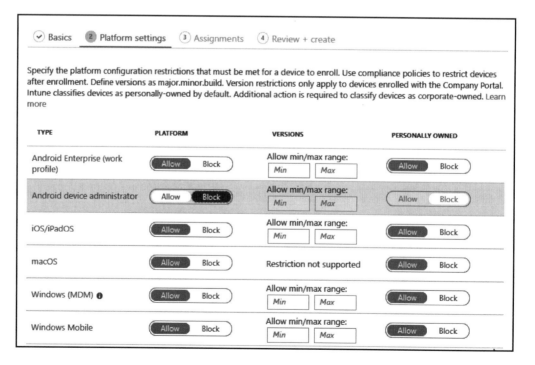

Once the platform settings are configured, you click **Next** and assign the restriction to specific groups and confirm the restriction settings.

Now that we've seen the capabilities of **Device type restrictions**, let's look at the device *limit* restrictions.

Device limit restrictions

By default, your users are restricted to enrolling five devices, but you can limit them to any number between 1 and 15:

1. To create a device limit restriction, go to **Azure | Device enrollment | Enrollment restrictions** and click **Create restriction**.
2. Choose **Device limit restriction** for the restriction type, and then name and describe the restriction as before.
3. Choose the maximum number of devices a user subject to this policy can enroll. Once you click **Next**, you can assign it to specific user groups. Refer to the following screenshot:

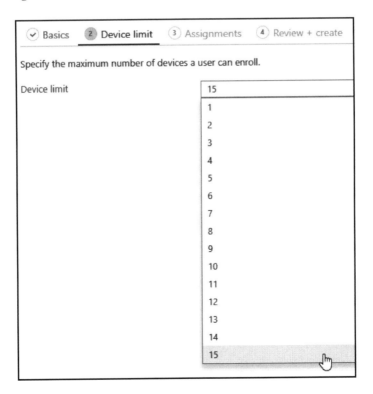

When finished assigning to groups, you'll click **Next**, review for accuracy, and then select **Create** to complete the restriction.

In the final section of this chapter, we took a look at how we can improve our device management by limiting users to enrolling specific device types and quantities. Let's now review what we've learned in this chapter.

Summary

In this chapter, we covered the following exam topics:

- Planning for MDM
- Configuring MDM integration with Azure AD
- Setting an MDM authority
- Setting device enrollment limits for users

By properly planning for MDM, you're making sure devices accessing an organization's resources are compliant and reduce the risk of data loss. Intune has many settings for customizing the criteria for and actions in response to compliance (or lack thereof).

Configuring MDM with Azure AD allows you the ability to manage AD-registered and AD-joined devices from within Azure AD. Users are also able to automatically enroll their devices. As an administrator, you have the ability to configure a hybrid Azure AD join, which provides the ability to use group policies on devices.

MDM authorities include Intune Standalone, Intune co-management, or Office 365 MDM. Note that O365 MDM still requires Intune.

You may wish to limit the number or type of devices any one user is able to enroll. This would help ensure you don't exceed licensing limits or grant access to unsupported device types. Placing a limit also encourages users to be selective in how broadly they're accessing company resources and reduces the number of potential data loss endpoints.

In the next chapter, we'll take what we've learned here and dive in a little deeper. We'll be covering planning for device compliance, configuring device compliance policies, and creating conditional access policies.

Questions

1. You need to configure your device management settings so that users cannot access company resources and data using devices running Android 7.0 or earlier. Which of the following must you configure to accomplish this task (select all that apply)?

    A. Conditional access policy
    B. Compliance policy
    C. Terms and conditions users must accept
    D. Custom configuration policy

2. Your Windows 10 and Android device users aren't having issues self-enrolling their devices, but your Apple users get an error. Given this information, which of the following is most likely the cause?

    A. Users don't have Intune subscription licenses assigned.
    B. Apple Configurator profile is bad.
    C. Apple MDM push certificate isn't present or valid.
    D. Users don't have valid Apple IDs.

Further reading

- **Planning for MDM**:
    - *Intune deployment planning, design, and implementation guide*: https://docs.microsoft.com/en-us/intune/planning-guide.
    - *Apply features and settings on your devices using device profiles in Microsoft Intune*: https://docs.microsoft.com/en-us/intune/device-profiles.

- **Configuring MDM integration with Azure AD**:
    - *How to: Plan your Azure AD join implementation*: https://docs.microsoft.com/en-us/azure/active-directory/devices/azureadjoin-plan
    - *How To: Plan your hybrid Azure Active Directory join implementation*: https://docs.microsoft.com/en-us/azure/active-directory/devices/hybrid-azuread-join-plan

- *Quickstart: Set up automatic enrollment for Windows 10 devices*: https://docs.microsoft.com/en-us/intune/quickstart-setup-auto-enrollment
- *What is a device identity?*: https://docs.microsoft.com/en-us/azure/active-directory/devices/overview

- **Setting an MDM authority**:
  - *Set the mobile device management authority*: https://docs.microsoft.com/en-au/intune/mdm-authority-set

- **Setting device enrollment limits for users**:
  - *Set enrollment restrictions*: https://docs.microsoft.com/en-us/intune/enrollment-restrictions-set

Managing Device Compliance 2

In Chapter 1, *Implementing Mobile Device Management (MDM)*, we introduced you to mobile device management, and we started looking at device compliance. In this chapter, we will cover device compliance in more detail and prepare you for exam questions regarding setting up compliance and conditional access policies.

Device compliance is determined by the settings that the administrators configure in the admin portal. For any devices – BYOD or otherwise – to be allowed access to company apps, services, and data, they must meet a set of criteria.

In this chapter, you'll learn about the following exam topics:

- Planning for device compliance
- Configuring device compliance policies
- Designing, creating, and managing conditional access policies

Planning for device compliance

Before you begin creating policies, take a moment to consider all of your options and identify which configurations best suit your organizational compliance needs. You'll consider a number of factors, including the restrictions we set up in Chapter 1, *Implementing Mobile Device Management (MDM)*, and the types of responses that are appropriate at different levels of device compliance.

Typically, you'll create a compliance policy and *then* create a conditional access policy using the compliance status from the first policy as a determining characteristic, for example, *if Device A is compliant, allow access to SharePoint*. Let's take a look at this process:

1. In Intune, navigate to **Device Compliance**. From here, you can view or create compliance policies based on individual device platforms. After navigating to **Device Compliance**, select **Policies | Create Policy** to begin a new policy. The initial setup screen resembles the following, where you'll select a platform to which the policy will apply:

2. Once you've configured the compliance policy, you can create conditional access policies in Azure AD, which require those compliance policies to be met so that a device or app can be granted access to organizational data.

To plan for the implementation of compliance and conditional access policies, answer the following questions:

- Which groups of users may require more or less restrictive policies?
- On which platforms will your managed devices operate (Android, Windows 10, and so on)?
- What action(s) should be taken when a device is identified as non-compliant, and how long can a device be non-compliant before that happens?

We now know how to set up compliance policies based on device platforms and that we will likely use the compliance status that's determined by the policy to allow or disallow access via a conditional access policy. Now, let's configure a full compliance policy.

Configuring device compliance policies

Device compliance policies differ from conditional access policies in that they identify devices that are compliant or not, but do not restrict/allow access to organizational resources on their own.

Policy options

Each platform has different policy configuration options, but most share some commonalities, as shown in the following screenshot:

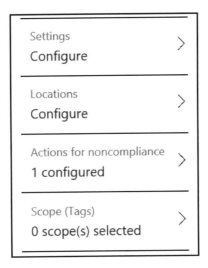

Let's go over these different options:

- **Settings**:
    - **Device Health**, including **Google Play Protect** settings:

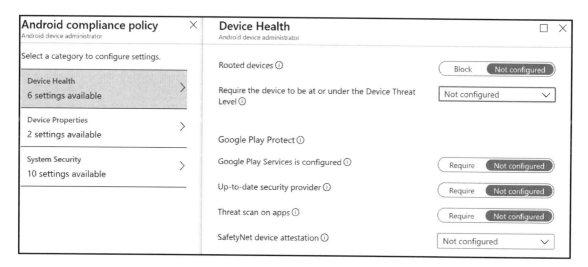

- **Device Properties**, specifically the minimum and maximum OS versions:

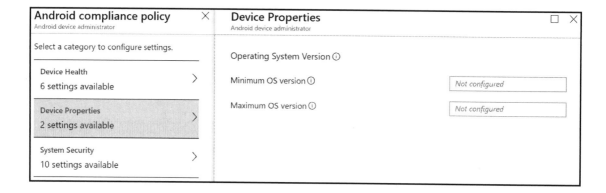

- **System Security**, such as password requirements and app restrictions:

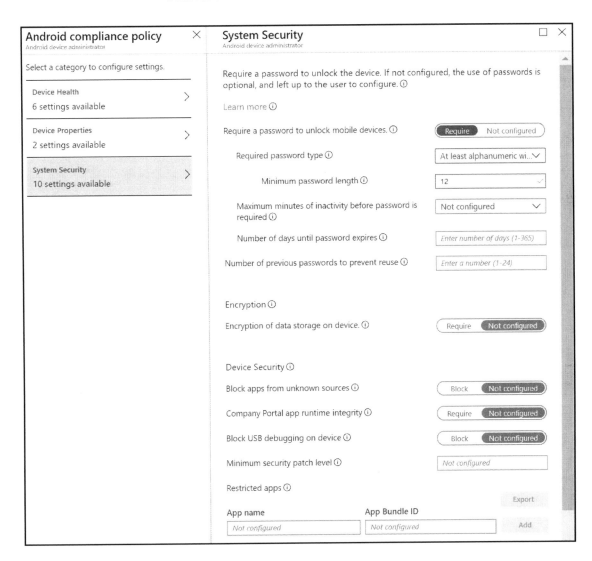

Your available settings will differ on each platform. For example, in the preceding screenshot, for Android, there are 10 settings available. However, for Windows 10 devices, we have additional options, such as minimum password length, as shown in the following screenshot:

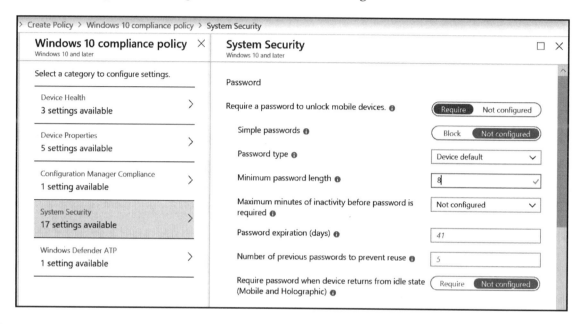

- **Locations**:
    - You can restrict your devices to specific locations:

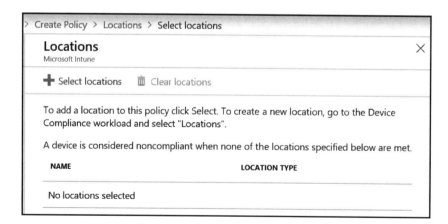

Because we haven't created any locations yet, we can't select them for use in the policy. To create a location, follow these steps:

1. Go to **Device Compliance**, select **Locations**, and click on **+ Create**. Fill in the specifications, as shown in the following screenshot.
2. Once the locations have been configured, select **Policies** from the left-hand pane to resume the creation/modification of device compliance policies:

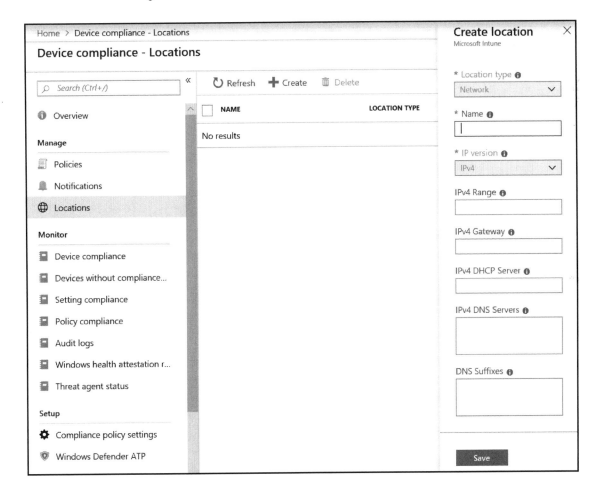

- **Actions for noncompliance**:
    - From here, you can decide on what happens if a device is deemed noncompliant. By default, the device will just be marked as noncompliant and no further action will be taken. However, you can configure the policy so that it emails the user or even remotely locks the device if these issues aren't resolved within so many days of being identified as noncompliant.
    - If you do add additional actions, they will be listed in the order they will be executed in, based on the **Schedule** field of each action where you've specified the number of days to wait:

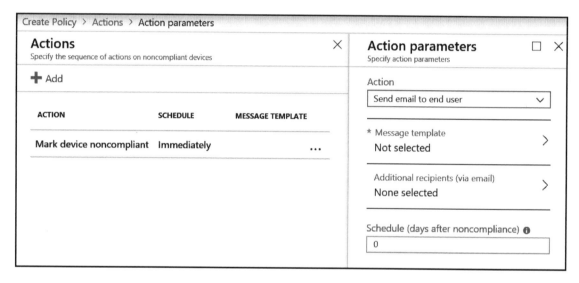

- **Scope (Tags)**:
    - Scope tags allow you to specify which profiles, policies, and devices admins have the ability to see and manage. For example, you could restrict a **Midwest Admin** group to only manage devices and policies with a **Midwest** scope tag assigned to them. In this section, we're considering this **Scope (Tags)** functionality as it relates to viewing and managing compliance policies.

You can find out more about scope tags at `https://docs.microsoft.com/en-us/intune/scope-tags`.

Now that we've taken a look at many of the options we'll need to configure in our policy, let's create one.

Creating a compliance policy

Now that you understand some of the policy options, follow these steps to create your first policy:

1. Go to Intune (go to `devicemanagement.microsoft.com` or `portal.azure.com` and search for `Intune`).
2. Click on **Device compliance** in the left-hand pane.
3. Under **Manage**, select **Policies**.
4. Select **+ Create Policy**:

5. Name and describe the policy and select the particular platform this policy will apply to:

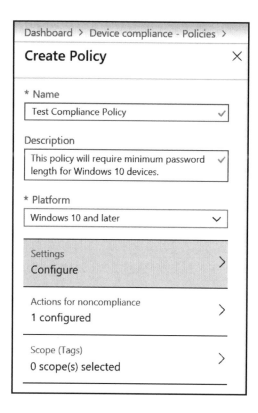

6. Select **Configure** to begin adjusting the platform-specific settings that are available. These indicate whether a device is compliant for your organization. Each platform will differ in terms of the available options:

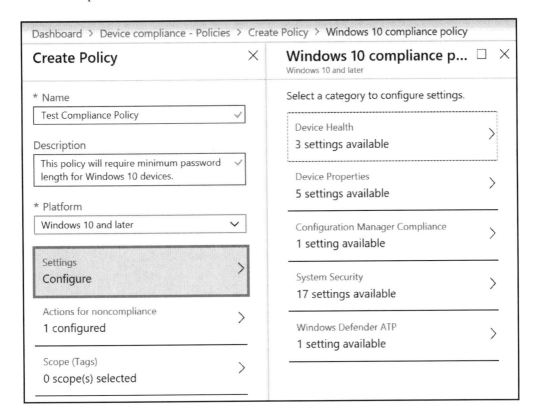

7. In this example, we'll select **System Security** so that we can have a minimum password length of 12 characters for our Windows 10 devices:

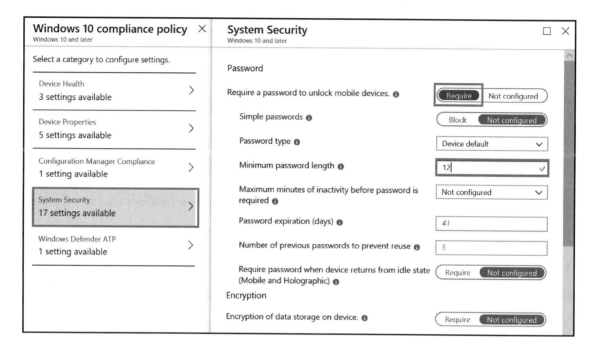

8. When finished, click **OK** until you're back in the **Create Policy** pane, as shown in *step 5*.

9. Now, click on **Actions for noncompliance** to choose what happens when a device does not meet the requirements you've just configured. By default, the device is marked as noncompliant. You can add additional actions and set them to take effect after a certain duration if you wish:

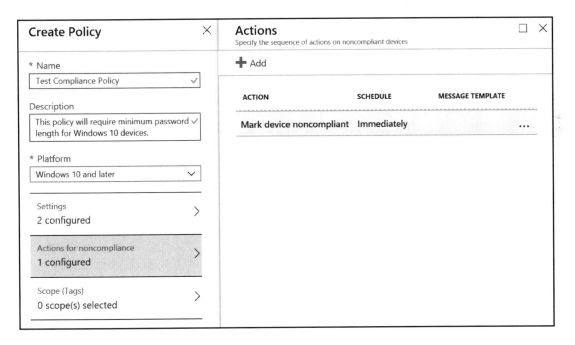

10. Click **OK** until you're back to just the **Create Policy** pane again. If you wish to configure **Scope (Tags)**, you may. Otherwise, click **Create**:

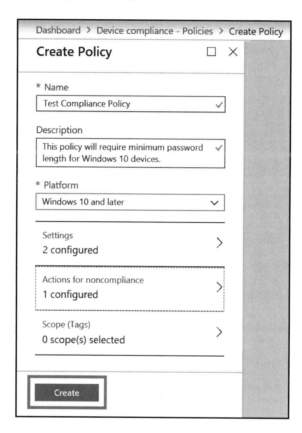

11. Once created, you'll be presented with a monitoring page for the new policy, along with a reminder that you need to assign the policy to a group (or multiple groups) before it can take effect. Click **Assignments**:

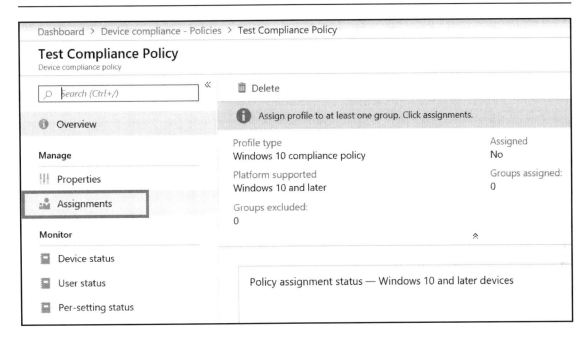

12. Select the user or device group(s) to be subjected to this new device compliance policy. You can assign it to all groups *except* certain groups by using the **Exclude** option; otherwise, use the **Include** option to target specific groups:

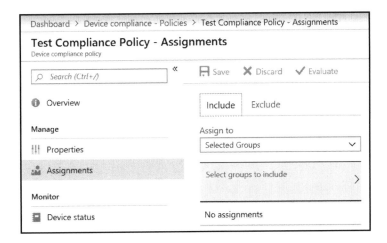

13. Click **Save** when you're finished.
14. If you need to modify the policy later, repeat *steps 1-3* and then select the policy you wish to modify.
15. Click on **Properties**. Here, you'll be presented with the configuration options for the policy, just like in *step 5*:

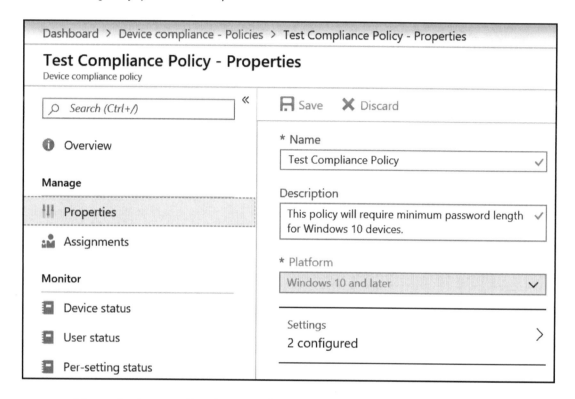

After selecting a policy from **Device compliance**, you'll be able to view the reports of devices and the users who are subject to the policy and its current status.

16. You can check additional reports, such as **Device compliance**, under
    the **Monitor** heading at any time to get a snapshot of your overall compliance:

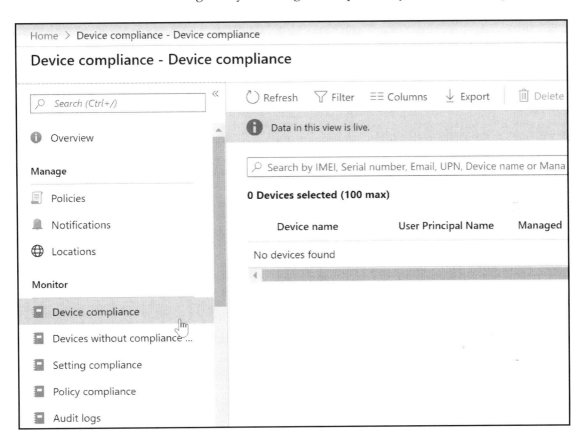

Mobile device compliance in Intune does not allow or restrict access
unless you use Azure AD's conditional access function. Without
conditional access, mobile device compliance still provides you with some
functionality, such as remote locking, running the reports of non-
compliant managed devices (jailbroken systems, unencrypted systems,
old operating systems, and so on), and emailing users with reminders to
make their device(s) compliant.

Now, we have our first compliance policy. In the next section, we'll explore how
conditional access policies in Azure AD complement the compliance policy you configured
in Intune.

Designing, creating, and managing conditional access policies

Conditional access can be granted via an Azure Active Directory premium license. Intune's mobile device compliance and **mobile application management** (**MAM**) solutions work with Azure so that you can allow or block access to organization resources based on a device or app's characteristics and behaviors. Any compliance policy can be used as a condition in a conditional access policy.

In the following sections, we'll look at what we can when we're designing a conditional access policy, how to create a policy, and how to manage them once they've been created.

Designing conditional access policies

When designing conditional access policies for mobile devices, you're trying to find the most appropriate configuration in order to implement corporate policy within Azure AD and Intune. There are many customizations for conditional access policies, including using everything we've discussed that can make a device compliant (or not) as a condition.

When you create a policy, you're presented with two sets of settings:

- Assignments:
    - Users and groups
    - Cloud apps or actions
    - Conditions
- Access controls:
    - Grant
    - Session

Assignments

Beneath *Assignments*, you'll find three configurable subcategories per policy:

- Users and groups (who does it apply to)
- Cloud apps or actions (what does it apply to)
- Conditions (when does it apply)

Let's start by taking a look at users and groups.

Users and groups

The **Users and groups** section is where you specify whether a conditional access policy will apply to all users, a subset of users (a group), or a group of devices. This is where, for example, you can configure external user access restrictions or force certain roles, such as app administrators, to have more restrictive authentication settings:

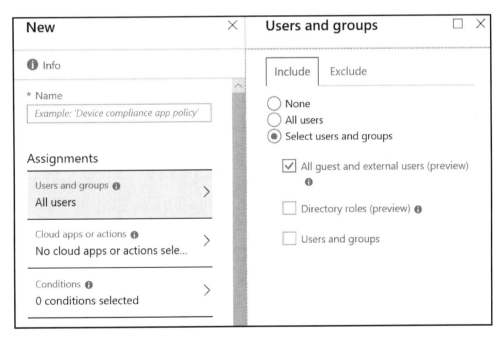

Next, we'll look at cloud apps or actions.

Cloud apps or actions

Under the **Cloud apps or actions** section, you can set policies that can apply to or exclude certain apps, such as a Teams- or SharePoint-specific policy.

Keep in mind that, when creating Teams-specific policies, Teams depend on other apps and services, including Stream, SharePoint, and OneDrive. This means that the user experience could be severely affected by a policy that doesn't take that into consideration:

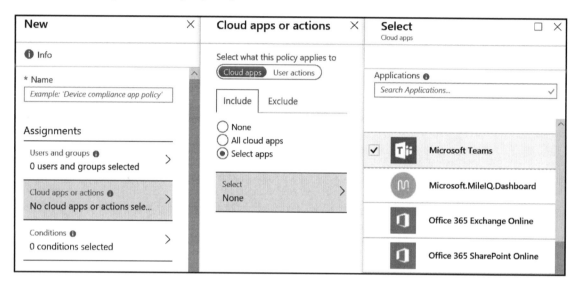

The last thing we need to look at in the **Assignments** section of our policy is conditions.

Conditions

The **Conditions** section allows you to choose when your policy will apply. You can do this by specifying client sign-in risk, device platforms, locations, client apps, and device state requirements:

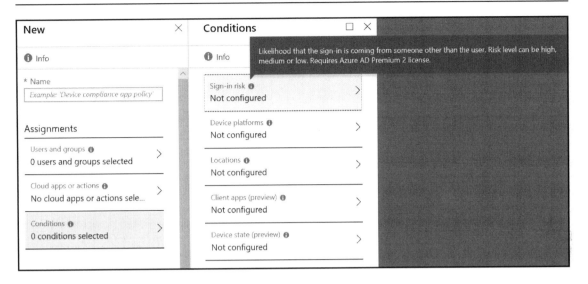

For example, you may wish to configure **Conditions | Client apps (preview)** when your company wants to enforce MAM, thereby disallowing copying and pasting from Outlook to other apps. By disabling Outlook access via the **Browser**, you can force users to use a client or mobile app in which you're able to enforce that MAM procedure:

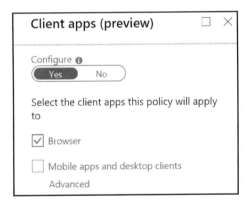

Under **Device state (preview)**, you can configure your policy so that it excludes devices that have been marked as compliant via one of the device compliance policies you configured in Intune:

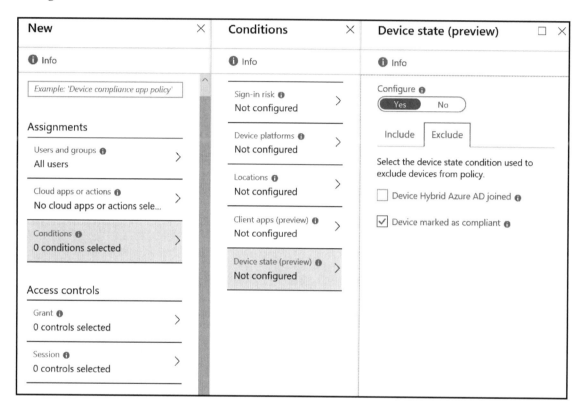

You may be asked to create conditional access policies that meet a variety of needs. For example, you could create a conditional access policy based on the following requirements:

- Network access control
- Device or sign-in risk
- Device compliance (platforms, OS version, personal versus corporate, and so on)
- Trusted locations versus untrusted locations
- **Multi-factor authentication (MFA)** setup

Based on these device and context characteristics (and many more), you can restrict access to on-premises emails, cloud apps and services, and even VPN access.

Now, we're ready to look at the **Access controls** section of the policy.

Access controls

Access controls allow you to specify whether the assignments you've configured are meant to allow or restrict access and whether there are additional caveats to that access. You can configure two sections, **Grant** and **Session**:

- **Grant**: With grants, you can specify additional requirements that must be met or block access entirely. You could choose all of the following, or require that just one of them is met:
  - Require MFA
  - Require device compliance
  - Require hybrid AD joined device
  - Require approved client app
  - Require app protection policy
- **Session**: With sessions, you can permit limited or full experiences in SharePoint and Exchange by passing device information to the apps, or force more frequent reauthentication. You're able to configure each of the following controls:
  - Use app enforced restrictions (SharePoint Online and Exchange Online only)
  - Use conditional access app control
  - Sign-in frequency
  - Persistent browser session

First, we'll look at whether or not we should block or allow access. We can do this in the **Grant** section.

Grant

When you select **Grant**, you need to decide whether you're using this policy to block or permit access based on the conditions you're specifying. If you're pairing this with a device compliance policy, this is where you could check the box for **Require device to be marked as compliant**:

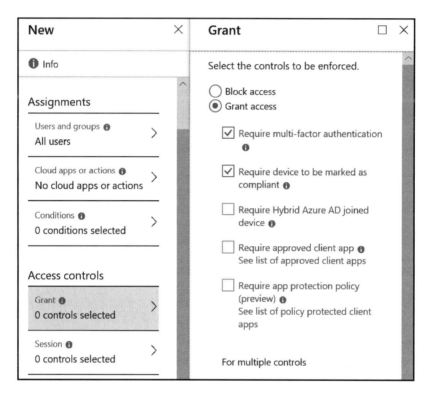

Next, let's look at **Session**.

Session

The **Session** section allows you to limit cloud app experiences or restrict authentication sessions. For example, you can configure your policy so that users are asked to sign in again after 30 days (the default is 90 days) if the policy applies to the user:

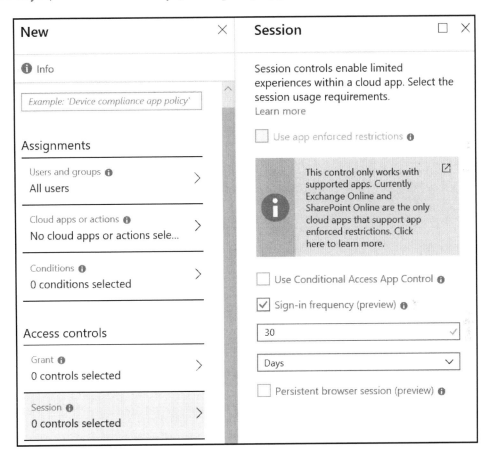

Now that we've taken a look at the basic components of conditional access policies, we're ready to create our own.

Creating conditional access policies

To start creating conditional access policies go to Azure (`portal.azure.com`), navigate to Azure AD, and select **Conditional Access** from under **Security**. You can also search from within Azure for conditional access and select the first result under **Services**:

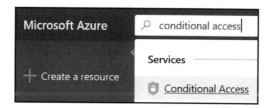

1. Select **New policy**:

2. Name your policy:

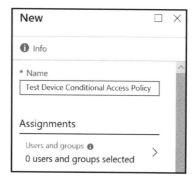

3. Under **Assignments**, click **Users and groups** to select who or which groups this policy will apply to:

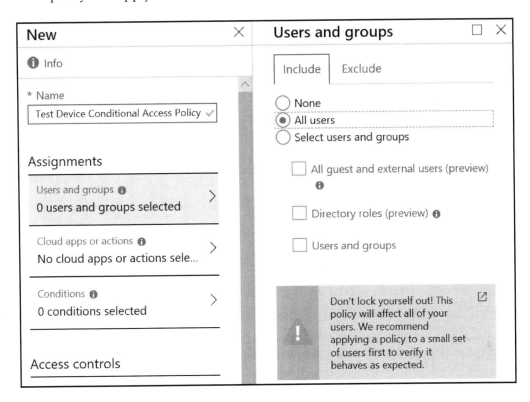

4. Select **Cloud apps or actions** and choose which abilities you're allowing or restricting. In my example, I'm allowing all users to access forms and flows conditionally:

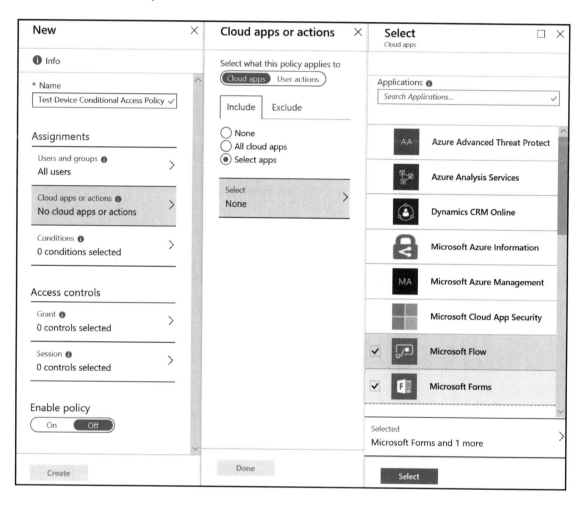

5. Now, you can configure the **Conditions** for this policy, such as excluding instances in which users are attempting to access the apps/actions from a trusted location:

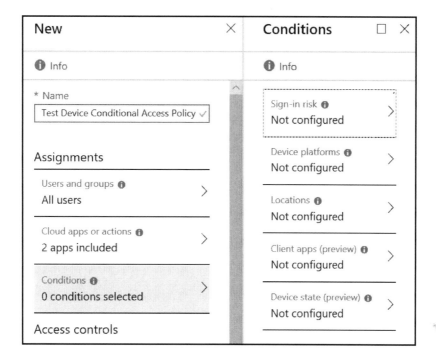

6. Under **Access controls**, select **Grant** and choose whether this policy is granting or blocking access if the conditions are met. In my example, I'm simply saying **Grant access** to forms and flows to all users as long as the device is marked as compliant. Click **Select** to save these details:

7. If you're ready to enable the policy immediately, toggle **Enable policy** and click **Create**. You can always enable it later if you're not quite ready:

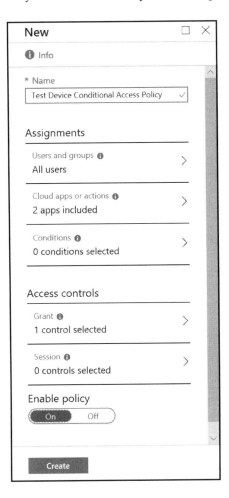

8. When finished, use the **What If** button from the conditional access landing page to test the impact and effectiveness of your policies for particular users under specific circumstances:

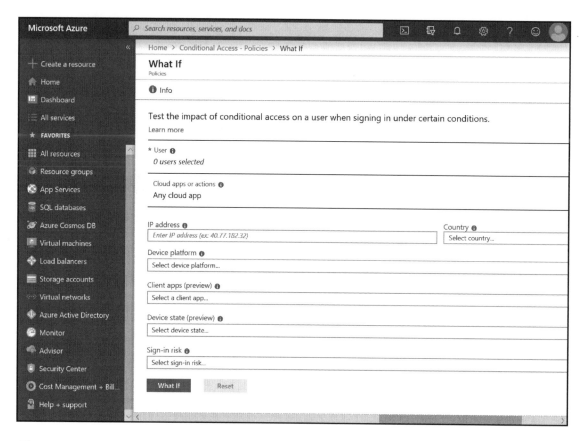

Chances are, once your policies have been created, you'll want to check their performance and make sure they're behaving as intended. To do this, we need to manage our policies.

Managing conditional access policies

At any time, you may need to check on the performance or status of one of the policies you've created, or make adjustments to additional settings. Let's look at how we can view and administer our conditional access policies:

1. From the **Conditional Access - Policies** landing page, you can review all of your policies and see which are enabled at a glance. You can select any of them to revise them, or use the ellipses next to a policy to delete it:

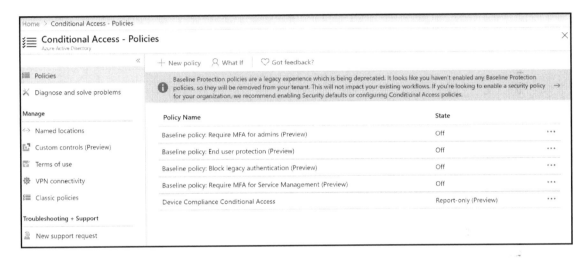

2. On the left-hand side, you'll see additional management tools for adding and managing **Named locations** (some of which can be trusted locations that are used in conditional access policies):

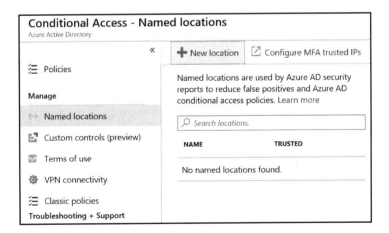

3. If you select **+New location** you can enter IP ranges or countries/regions to include in that new named location. You may also upload a TXT file with a list of IP ranges, one per line, using the **Upload** button:

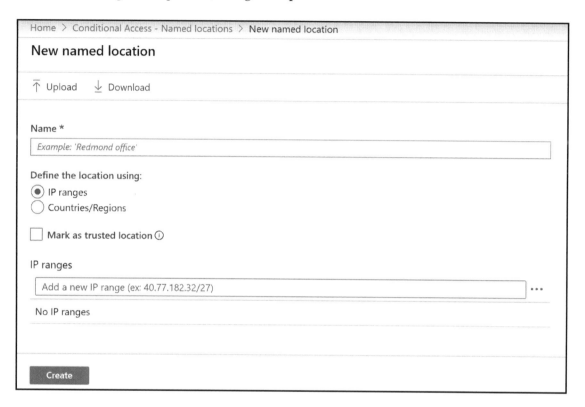

Another management option is configuring the terms of use for users to accept prior to accessing the company resources, which will be subject to conditional access policies.

You can also configure always-on VPN deployment for devices that meet your conditional access policy criteria.

In this section, we've taken a look at how we can further manage our conditional access policies. In the next chapter, we'll explore a few more device usage-specific topics, such as security and app deployment.

Summary

In this chapter, we've covered how to plan for device compliance, how to configure device compliance policies, and how to design, create, and manage conditional access policies.

By planning for device compliance, we were introduced to compliance policy's roles in device access restrictions. Device compliance policies allow us to define what makes a device compliant and can help us with reporting or making notifications on the compliance status. Conditional access policies can look at our compliance policies and allow or block access to devices based on their compliance status.

In the next chapter, we're going to begin looking at the device experience, that is, the apps and security on the device itself.

Questions

1. Requirement: You need to make sure iOS users are accessing your company's data from a device running the latest operating system, and block access if they are not.
    Solution: You create a device compliance policy in Intune.
    Does this solution meet the specified requirement?

    A. Yes
    B. No

2. You need to allow Tokyo employees access to company resources from mobile devices, but only when they're connected to the company's network. What should you configure?

    A. An advanced threat management setting
    B. A device compliance policy
    C. A data loss prevention policy
    D. A conditional access policy

Further reading

- **Planning for device compliance**:
    - *You can set rules on devices to allow access to resources in your organization using Intune*: https://docs.microsoft.com/en-us/intune/device-compliance-get-started
    - *Learn how to monitor Intune device compliance policies*: https://docs.microsoft.com/en-us/intune/compliance-policy-monitor
- **Configuring device compliance policies**:
    - *Create a compliance policy in Microsoft Intune*: https://docs.microsoft.com/en-us/intune/create-compliance-policy
    - *Use Locations (network fence) in Intune*: https://docs.microsoft.com/en-us/intune/use-network-locations
    - *Quickstart: Create a password compliance policy for Android devices*: https://docs.microsoft.com/en-us/intune/quickstart-set-password-length-android
    - *Quickstart: Send notifications to noncompliant devices*: https://docs.microsoft.com/en-us/intune/quickstart-send-notification
    - *Automate email and add actions for noncompliant devices in Intune*: https://docs.microsoft.com/en-us/intune/actions-for-noncompliance
- **Designing, creating, and managing conditional access policies**:
    - *Learn about conditional access and Intune*: https://docs.microsoft.com/en-us/intune/conditional-access
    - *What are access controls in Azure Active Directory Conditional Access? Session controls*: https://docs.microsoft.com/en-us/azure/active-directory/conditional-access/controls#session-controls
    - *Always On VPN deployment for Windows Server and Windows 10*: https://docs.microsoft.com/en-us/windows-server/remote/remote-access/vpn/always-on-vpn/deploy/always-on-vpn-deploy

Planning for Devices and Apps 3

Being able to provision licenses for purchased apps through a customized app store is one component of managing your enterprise data and security. You're effectively able to select which apps are (and aren't) allowed for users to install on their own, using a customized store you set up for them. And for apps that are not self-service downloads/installs, you're able, as an administrator, to deploy apps through other methods to devices.

Once users have apps connecting to company resources and data, you can use **mobile application management** (**MAM**) to make sure users are responsibly accessing and interacting with content. For example, you could disable copy/paste functionality for Office apps to make it more difficult for data to leave your environment.

This chapter provides information about deploying apps and utilizing MAM, specifically looking at the following exam topics:

- Creating and configuring Microsoft Store for Business
- Planning app deployment
- Planning device co-management
- Planning device monitoring
- Planning for device profiles
- Planning for MAM
- Planning mobile device security

Let's start with understanding Microsoft Store for Business, an option that enables users to choose certain apps for installation on their device(s).

Creating and configuring Microsoft Store for Business

Microsoft Store for Business provides you with the ability to centrally manage license acquisition, billing, and assignment for apps in your organization. Apps with online licenses also stay up to date and install cleanly, meaning less administrative work throughout the entire life cycle of the app and its usage.

To create and configure Microsoft Store for Business, you'll need to complete a few steps. In the following examples, I'll be using Intune as my selected MDM tool. If you require advanced functionality such as managing images as well, you may have a different third-party MDM tool of choice:

1. Create your private store.
2. Set your MDM solution in Microsoft Store.
3. Configure synchronization in Intune and synchronize apps.

Now, let's look at each of these steps more closely.

Creating your private store

Perform the following steps to create a private store:

1. Sign into Microsoft Store as an admin at `https://businessstore.microsoft.com`.
2. Click **Private store** and **Activate private store**:

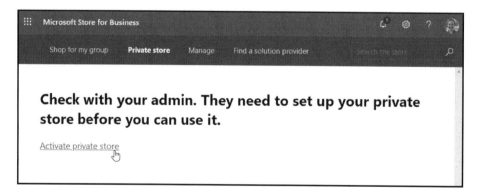

3. Accept the services agreement after reviewing.
4. Your store is now created, and you can begin purchasing apps and organizing them into collections:
   1. Click **Shop for my group** to add apps.
   2. Click the name of your private store from the menu to organize purchased apps into collections that make sense in your organization (Office apps, productivity, data analytics, and so on).

Next, we'll configure our store to recognize our MDM solution, and then configure our MDM solution (Intune, in this example) to synchronize from Microsoft Store for Business.

Setting your MDM solution in Microsoft Store

Perform the following steps to set your MDM solution:

1. Sign into Microsoft Store as an admin at `https://businessstore.microsoft.com`.
2. Click **Manage**.
3. Click **Settings** | **Distribute** | **Activate** (next to your MDM solution):

From this page, you can also configure a custom private store name. Next we'll configure and finalize the synchronization.

Configuring synchronization in Intune and synchronizing apps

Perform the following steps to configure synchronization in Intune:

1. Sign in to Intune at `https://devicemanagement.microsoft.com/` and click on **Client apps**.
2. Click **Microsoft Store for Business** under **Setup**.
3. Click **Enable**.
4. Click **Save**:

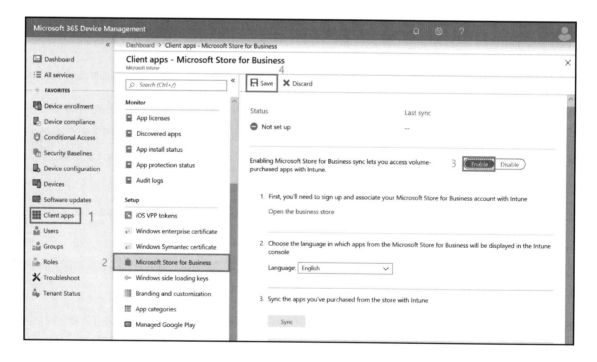

5. After saving, the **Sync** button should now be available to synchronize purchased apps, as follows:

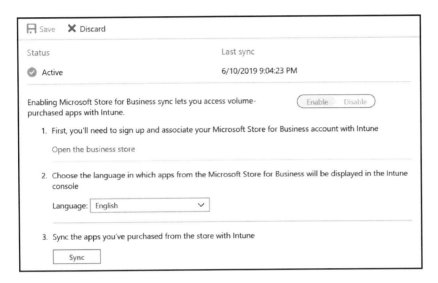

6. To confirm synchronization and review available licenses, go to **App licenses** under **Monitor** to see what has synchronized:

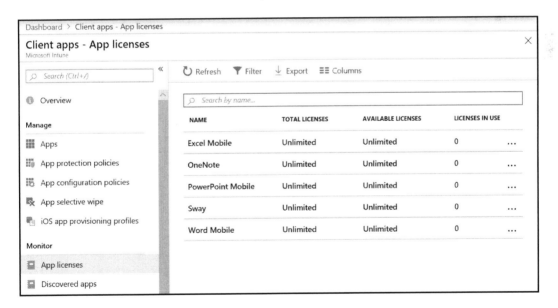

If you're ready to assign, you can select **Apps** under **Manage**. We'll cover assigning apps a little later in this chapter.

 You can learn more about managing Microsoft Store apps with Intune at `https://docs.microsoft.com/en-us/intune/windows-store-for-business`.

Next we'll look at options and considerations for deploying apps.

Planning app deployment

In thinking about app deployment, you should consider whether you'll be deploying apps to devices other than Windows 10 devices. If exclusively Windows 10 devices, Microsoft Store for Business is sufficient for deploying apps. But if you are other platforms such as iOS or Android devices, you'll need to use Microsoft Store integrated with Intune.

With that in mind, you have three basic deployment options when it comes to distributing apps from the Microsoft Store:

- Use a management tool
- Make apps available via your private store
- Assign apps directly to employees

Let's explore each of these methods.

Using a management tool

You can use a third-party management tool to distribute apps so long as it's configured in Azure **Active Directory** (**AD**) (in the same Azure instance as Microsoft Store). You can either configure **offline deployment** (downloading the app and its license for deployment through your MDM) or **online deployment** (connecting to the Microsoft Store management services for deployment).

 Take a closer look at using a management tool by checking out the documentation at `https://docs.microsoft.com/en-us/microsoft-store/distribute-apps-with-management-tool`.

Making apps available via your private store

To make apps available through your private store, follow these steps:

1. From Microsoft Store for Business, click **Manage** | **Products & services**.
2. Select the name of the app you're assigning.
3. Click **Private store availability**.
4. Choose whether all users can see the app in the private store, or if only specific AD groups can:

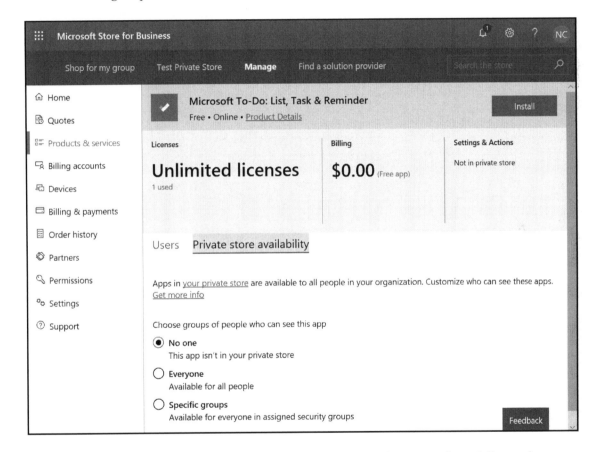

 You can learn more about distributing apps via your private Microsoft Store for Business at `https://docs.microsoft.com/en-us/microsoft-store/distribute-apps-from-your-private-store`.

Assigning apps directly to employees

To assign apps to specific users, follow these steps:

1. From Microsoft Store for Business, click **Manage | Products & services**.
2. Select the name of the app you're assigning.
3. Search for and select user(s).
4. Click **Assign to Users** as seen in the following screenshot:

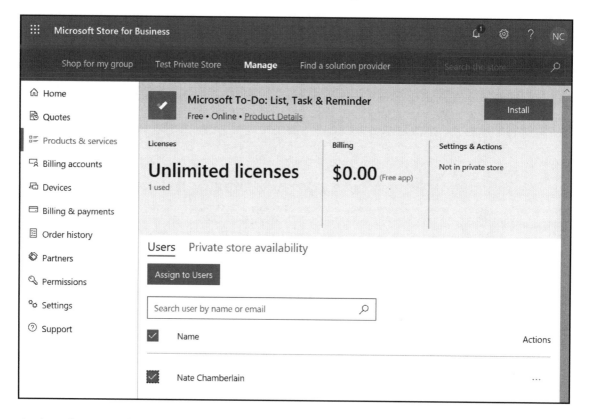

Assigned users will receive an email with instructions to install.

 Learn more about assigning apps to employees at `https://docs.microsoft.com/en-us/microsoft-store/assign-apps-to-employees`.

Next we'll learn about device co-management.

Planning device co-management

Co-management allows you to attach your existing **System Center Configuration Manager** (**SCCM**) deployment to Intune MDM to allow additional functionality such as conditional access, linking devices to Azure AD, remote restart or factory reset, and so on. These abilities come in handy when a user reports a device missing or stolen and you need to ensure the safety of corporate data on the device. And with co-management, you're getting the best of on-premises device management and cloud-based management.

Co-management requires SCCM and an EMS subscription. If you don't have EMS, you'll need an Azure AD premium license and Intune licenses for all users.

To begin setting up co-management, follow these steps:

1. Go to **System Center Configuration Manager** | **Administration** | **Cloud Services** | **Co-Management**.
2. Click **Configure co-management** to open the co-management onboarding wizard.
3. When you sign in to your Azure AD tenant through the wizard, you'll be asked if you want to automatically enroll existing Configuration Manager clients in Intune. You can choose **Pilot** or **All** for devices to enroll. **Pilot** will only enroll the devices you designate later as part of a pilot group; **All** will enroll all devices.
4. Configure workloads, deciding which workloads will be managed by Configuration Manager or Intune:
   - **Configuration Manager**: Continue managing in Configuration Manager
   - **Pilot Intune**: Continue managing in Configuration Manager except for items in the Pilot group (configured in the wizard)
   - **Intune**: Manage in Intune

Note the following table is not a recommendation, but an example of the choices you'll need to make when working through the co-management onboarding wizard. For each workload, you'll decide how you want it managed. The Xs signify the selection you'd be making in the wizard:

	Configuration Manager	Pilot Intune	Intune
Compliance policies			X
Device configuration	X		
Endpoint protection	X		
Resource access policies	X		

Client apps		X	
Office Click-to-Run apps		X	
Windows update policies		X	

If, after configuration, you choose to switch workloads from one to another, you'll need to make sure you've configured and deployed the workload in Intune first so that the workload is managed by a tool at all times. Once switched, the managed device will automatically synchronize the MDM policy from Intune.

 Learn more about enabling co-management at https://docs.microsoft. com/en-us/sccm/comanage/how-to-enable and more on switching workloads at https://docs.microsoft.com/en-us/sccm/comanage/how-to-switch-workloads.

We'll explore device monitoring in the next section.

Planning device monitoring

You can monitor devices via SCCM or Intune.

For co-managed devices, you can use the SCCM's co-management dashboard (**Monitoring | Co-management**). This allows you to monitor the following:

- Windows client OS distribution (Windows 7/8, Windows 10, and so on)
- Co-management status (eligible, scheduled, or enrolled)
- Co-management enrollment status (succeeded or failed)
- Enrollment error counts
- Workload transition (for those you're moving to Intune)

In Intune, you can monitor the following:

- Device compliance (**Intune | Device Compliance | Overview**) shows the following:
    - Device compliance status
    - Devices without compliance policies
    - Policy compliance (how many devices are compliant/not compliant per policy)

- Device enrollment (**Intune** | **Device enrollment** | **Overview**) shows the following:
  - Enrollment failures by OS (Android, iOS, Windows, and so on).
  - Top enrollment failures weekly.
  - Select **Incomplete user enrollments** under **Monitor** to view a breakdown of initiated and incomplete enrollments over time.

Device profiles help us better manage and update devices. We'll look at them next.

Planning for device profiles

Device profiles contain configuration and compliance settings that can be pushed out to devices. For example, this ability allows administrators to bring organization-owned Windows devices to a compliant state in bulk, or to make adjustments to a *master* profile and implement them efficiently. These profiles contain such settings as the following:

- Administrative templates (groups of settings, similar to group policy)
- Device features
- Device restrictions
- Endpoint protection
- Identity protection
- VPN
- Wi-Fi
- Windows Defender ATP
- Windows Information Protection

Device profiles are also available to be configured for iOS and Android devices. These device profiles may include permission to use AirPrint printers in the organization, email profile configurations, Wi-Fi or VPN access, and more.

Devices that aren't personally owned or used for work by a single individual may also be managed by device profiles, such as an Android device used as a single-purpose kiosk for which the device profile would restrict web access, or app installations/usage outside the primary purpose.

Take a high-detail look at options and templates you can configure for device profiles at `https://docs.microsoft.com/en-us/intune/device-profiles`.

Let's look at how we assign profiles to devices.

Assigning profiles

Follow these steps to assign profiles:

1. Go to **Intune** (devicemanagement.microsoft.com).
2. Click on **Device configuration** | **Profiles**. From here you can assign an existing profile by selecting it, or you can create a new one and assign it after setup. Either way, after selecting an existing or creating a new profile, proceed to *step 3*.
3. On the **Assignments** tab under **Manage**, you can assign the new or existing profile to all users or devices (or both), or specific groups as seen in the following screenshot:

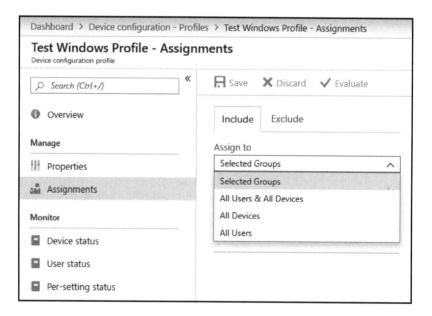

An easy way to restrict profiles to specific groups is to use scope tags. This would, for example, allow you to assign a device profile just to employees in South America or from a particular department.

Once device profiles are assigned, we can monitor them in Intune. Next we'll look at monitoring.

Monitoring profiles

You can monitor existing assignments and their statuses in Intune:

1. Go to **Intune** (devicemanagement.microsoft.com).
2. Click on **Device configuration** | **Profiles**. This lists all current profiles and their assignments.
3. Select a policy to view devices and the users it's assigned to:

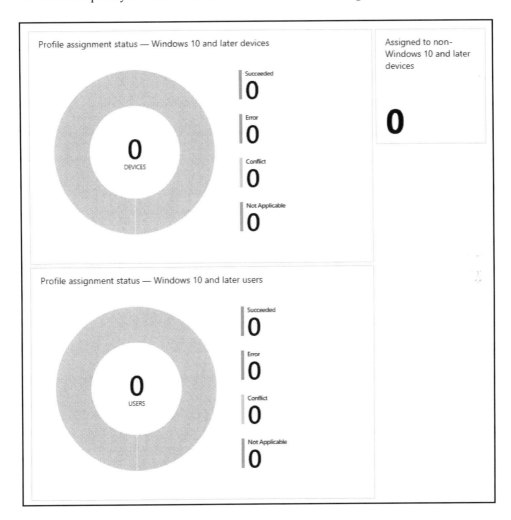

Lastly in this section, we'll look at what happens when multiple policies conflict.

Policy conflicts

As you're setting up device profiles and configurations, you may have two separate policies (or more) that meet the criteria for a single device. When multiple policies apply to the same user or device, they take precedence in the following order:

- **Compliance versus configuration policies**: Compliance policies overrule configuration policies.
- **Multiple compliance policies**: The most restrictive compliance policy wins.
- **Multiple configuration policies**: Intune will report the conflict and require manual resolution (**Device configuration | Assignment status**).

Let's look at considerations for planning MAM next.

Planning for MAM

We've explored MDM a bit, and now we'll cover its counterpart, MAM. MAM is popular in **bring your own device** (**BYOD**) scenarios and gives you the ability to manage *just* the apps on a device that connect to corporate data, and permits removing only the data associated with those managed apps. MDM, by comparison, manages the entirety of a device and permits removing all of a device's data.

The MAM policies you can create in **Intune | Client apps** could be app configuration policies or app protection policies. You'll also notice **App selective wipe** as an option, which allows you to remove *only* the corporate data from a user device.

App configuration policies assist in setting up apps on user devices, supplying information such as language and security settings for the app.

Creating an **app protection policy** allows you to restrict certain functions, such as copying information from a managed app (such as Outlook, demonstrated in the following screenshot) and pasting into a non-managed app (Gmail or Notes). The policy in the following screenshot also requires organizational data to be encrypted and allows syncing Outlook with the device's native contacts app:

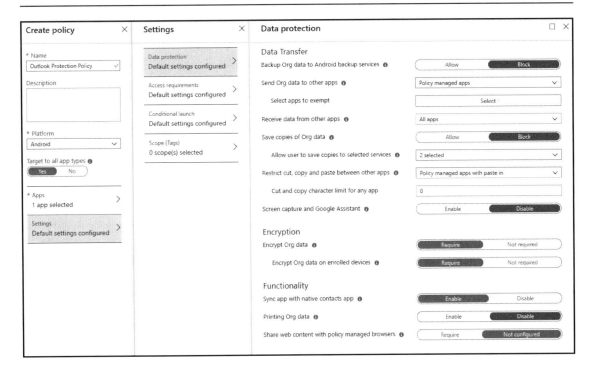

Check out the app life cycle for details on adding, deploying, configuring, protecting, and retiring apps through Intune at `https://docs.microsoft.com/en-us/intune/app-lifecycle`.

We'll end this chapter by looking at mobile device security capabilities.

Planning mobile device security

Intune provides many ways to protect your mobile devices, including many we've already discussed:

- Device compliance policies, such as minimum OS versions and jailbroken device detection
- Device configuration policies, such as restricting Bluetooth and configuring compliant apps
- Resetting passcodes and lock devices remotely

- Wiping data from devices remotely (**Intune** | **Devices** | **All devices** | **Select device** | **Wipe**)
- Retiring devices, removing all managed app data and configuration settings (leaving personal data intact)
- Managing **Multi-Factor Authentication** (**MFA**) and Windows Hello authentication settings

 You can learn more about your mobile device security options at `https://docs.microsoft.com/en-us/intune/device-protect`.

When planning mobile device security in your organization, it's important to keep in mind all of the possibilities we've discussed and find a combination of the abilities to secure your data and devices in the most efficient way. Before you begin actually building anything, it's a good idea to write it out and talk it through with others to make sure you're implementing a lean plan.

Summary

We've covered a lot of material in this chapter, including the following exam topic areas:

- Creating and configuring Microsoft Store for Business
- Planning app deployment
- Planning device co-management
- Planning device monitoring
- Planning for device profiles
- Planning for MAM
- Planning mobile device security

By configuring Microsoft Store for Business, you're preparing your organization for online or offline deployment of apps to Windows 10 devices and, when integrated with Intune, additional platforms such as iOS and Android.

Co-management gives you the *best of both worlds* when using SCCM and Intune. By opting for co-management, your SCCM-managed devices can benefit from additional Intune features such as conditional access and remote restart, or factory reset.

Monitor device enrollment, compliance, OS distribution, and more using SCCM's co-management dashboard and Intune's compliance and enrollment dashboards.

Device profiles allow you to *package* configurations for devices and to deploy them. These configurations could include Wi-Fi profiles or enabling/disabling device features such as built-in cameras.

MAM is a great solution for BYOD scenarios that allow you to manage the terms and conditions users agree to upon signing into apps allowing access to your organization's resources. You can allow your users to self-enroll their devices when they sign into apps, and you can define restrictions for appropriate usage to reduce the risk of data loss.

You have many options for implementing device security, including the compliance and configuration policies we've discussed, remote wiping and locking, and MFA. In the next chapter, we'll look at deploying Windows 10 in your environment.

Questions

1. Requirement: You're asked to provide a report of iOS devices that failed the enrollment process.
   Solution: You pull a report from SCCM's co-management dashboard.
   Does this meet the requirement?

   A. Yes
   B. No

2. Your company allows BYOD scenarios and employs MAM. When a user leaves the organization, you need to make sure their personal device no longer contains company data in managed apps and remove any Wi-Fi profile settings. When finished, the device shouldn't appear in Intune device management any longer. What is the appropriate action to take?

   A. Deploy a new device profile, then delete the device from **Intune | Devices | All Devices**
   B. Retire the device from **Intune | Devices | All Devices**
   C. Wipe the device from **Intune | Devices | All Devices**
   D. Delete the device from **Intune | Devices | All Devices**

Further reading

- **Creating and configuring Microsoft Store for Business**:
    - *Microsoft Store for Business and Education*: `https://docs.microsoft.com/en-us/microsoft-store/`
    - *Microsoft Store for Business and Microsoft Store for Education overview*: `https://docs.microsoft.com/en-us/microsoft-store/microsoft-store-for-business-overview`

- **Planning app deployment**:
    - *How to manage volume purchased apps from the Microsoft Store for Business with Microsoft Intune*: `https://docs.microsoft.com/en-us/intune/windows-store-for-business`

- **Planning device co-management**:
    - *How to prepare internet-based devices for co-management*: `https://docs.microsoft.com/en-us/sccm/comanage/how-to-prepare-Win10`

- **Planning for device profiles**:
    - *Assign user and device profiles in Microsoft Intune*: `https://docs.microsoft.com/en-us/intune/configuration/device-profile-assign`

- **Planning device monitoring**:
    - *Device management overview*: `https://docs.microsoft.com/en-us/intune/fundamentals/what-is-device-management`

- **Planning for MAM**:
    - *Frequently asked questions about MAM and app protection*: `https://docs.microsoft.com/en-us/intune/mam-faq`
    - *App configuration policies for Microsoft Intune*: `https://docs.microsoft.com/en-us/intune/apps/app-configuration-policies-overview`

- **Planning mobile device security**:
    - *Protect devices with Microsoft Intune*: `https://docs.microsoft.com/en-us/intune/device-protect`

4
Planning Windows 10 Deployment

In this chapter, we will look at how to configure **Windows as a Service** (**WaaS**) and create a plan for installing and maintaining Windows 10 on Enterprise devices as well as their ongoing upgrades on a servicing channel. You can use Upgrade Readiness and additional services to enhance your monitoring and administrative capabilities throughout the deployment and upgrade cycles.

Specifically, we'll be covering the following exam topics:

- Planning for WaaS
- Planning the appropriate Windows 10 Enterprise deployment method
- Analyzing Upgrade Readiness for Windows 10
- Evaluating and deploying additional Windows 10 Enterprise security features

Let's begin by planning for WaaS, that is, Microsoft's method of deploying ongoing OS feature updates on a regular basis.

Planning for WaaS

WaaS is a Windows 10-specific method for building, deploying, and servicing Windows 10 on organizational devices. It breaks away from traditional models for new OS releases by instead releasing features and important updates regularly, through different channels, to your organization's devices.

Let's take a look at how you, as an administrator, can work with WaaS.

Building and deploying

Previously, Windows was upgraded from one OS to the next, preserving apps and files, and could be minimally invasive to end users. Once a device is running Windows 10, users experience a similar transition from one build to the next through WaaS.

Administrators (or end users) can be a part of Windows Insider, which allows you to test-drive the latest features that are currently in development so you have enough time to gauge how it will impact your organization and its processes when it's released. Nobody likes to be surprised by a major change, so having someone in your organization responsible for staying abreast of these kinds of changes is a good idea.

You can also build *previews* into your release schedule, and identify pilot users who can be a part of the *Insider Preview* channel (refer to the *Servicing* section next) to make sure developing features won't cause significant obstacles for the organization.

Next, let's take a look at servicing and the various types of update you'll encounter.

Servicing

Servicing Windows 10 requires deploying updates within a reasonable time frame after being released. Organizations can choose to delay, or defer, a release, although the latest feature updates may be installed automatically prior to the end of service to ensure the security and functionality of the device.

Feature updates (a new functionality in Windows) can be previewed and tested while they're still being developed in *Insider Preview* builds of Windows; otherwise, an organization could pilot regular semiannual feature releases in groups (*deployment rings*) before deploying them across the entire organization. You'll also manage *quality updates*, dealing with security and non-security fixes.

Let's look at our options for servicing channels to understand when these feature updates can be received.

Servicing channels

There are two main servicing channels to consider when selecting an appropriate plan for the various devices you manage:

- **Semiannual channel**: Receive feature updates twice per year, approximately March and September:
  - March updates are serviced for 18 months after release.
  - September updates are serviced for 30 months after release.
- **Long-term servicing channel**: Receive feature updates every 2 to 3 years, supported for 10 years (this is ideal for kiosk machines, ATMs, and so on, which don't run Microsoft Office).

So, for example, you could follow an update plan such as this:

Deployment ring and servicing channel	Updates deferred for...	Explanation
Pre-release via Insider Preview	No deferment for feature or quality updates	Release features are currently in development to a select group.
Phase 1 via a semiannual channel (targeted)	No deferment for feature or quality updates	Release new features on day one, after Insider builds have run their course.
Phase 2 via a semiannual channel	90 days for feature updates, 7-10 days for quality updates	Let *phase 1* test out the new release and work through any initial bugs before pushing it out to the rest of the organization (this is ideal for critical systems).

Learn more about building your deployment rings at `https://docs.microsoft.com/en-us/windows/deployment/update/waas-deployment-rings-windows-10-updates`.

Now that you understand servicing channels and the types of update that will be sent through them, let's review the tools available to us for managing them.

Servicing tools

You can use any of the following tools to service Windows 10:

- Windows Update (cannot approve updates)
- Windows Update for Business (cannot approve updates)
- **Windows Server Update Services (WSUS)**
- **System Center Configuration Manager (SCCM)**

As you can see, if you need to approve updates before they're released to your devices, you'll want to use WSUS and SCCM.

In the next section, we'll explore choosing the best deployment method for your Enterprise scenario.

Planning for Windows 10 Enterprise deployment

You may have devices not yet running Windows 10, or new devices that still need to be initially configured. As we have already seen in this book, there are countless benefits to devices running Windows 10. One of the most prominent benefits is the end of major OS upgrades and the implementation of WaaS.

So, in thinking about moving to or installing Windows 10 on your organization's devices, there are two common methods that you can use to deploy it:

- Windows Autopilot (best for new devices)
- In-place upgrade (for devices running Windows 7 or 8.1)

In-place upgrades will preserve applications and settings. If you have an existing device running an earlier OS but just want a *clean install* (removing existing applications and data) you can perform a wipe-and-load before loading the OS.

 You can read more about all available deployment options, including less common methods for special cases, at `https://docs.microsoft.com/en-us/windows/deployment/windows-10-deployment-scenarios`.

Let's look a little more closely at these two deployment methods.

Windows Autopilot

The most common method for deploying Windows onto new devices is **Windows Autopilot**. It's a dynamic deploying method that allows your users to be mostly self-sufficient and, in just a few clicks, have their device set up with a customized **out-of-box experience (OOBE)** that you've configured in advance. The configuration replaces previous custom OS image building and deploying, and allows changes post-enrollment for apps, profiles, and policies.

You can start using Windows Autopilot by creating a deployment profile under **Microsoft Intune | Device enrollment | Windows enrollment | Deployment Profiles**:

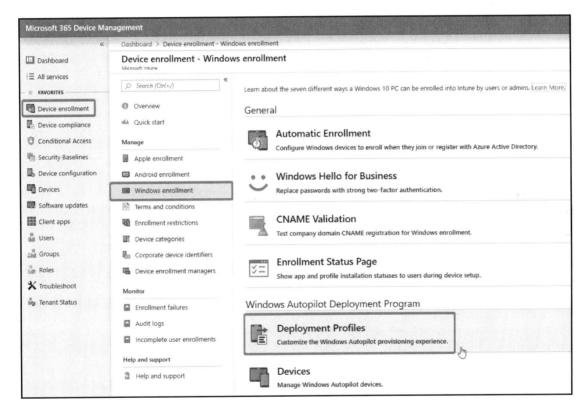

Windows Autopilot basically takes care of updates with very little end user interaction. There are two deployment modes available for OOBE:

- User-driven deployment (the device is associated with the user who is enrolling it)
- Self-deployment (not associated with a user, such as kiosks)

Be sure to configure your company branding in Azure AD to improve the user experience during Autopilot and prevent any errors. Learn how to add branding at `https://docs.microsoft.com/en-us/azure/active-directory/fundamentals/customize-branding`.

In the following screenshot, you can see the configuration screen for the OOBE page when creating a Windows Autopilot deployment profile:

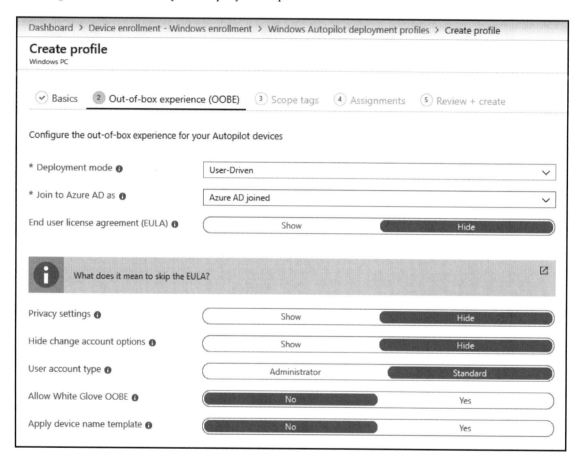

You can also reduce the time a user has to spend enrolling their device via Autopilot by utilizing white glove deployment. White glove deployment is where IT staff or a vendor/partner handle most of the work devoted to configuring the device in advance, and the receiving user will only have a few final steps to walk through before their device is fully provisioned and they're able to use their device more quickly.

> Read more about these two OOBE Windows Autopilot deployment methods at `https://docs.microsoft.com/en-us/windows/deployment/windows-autopilot/user-driven` and `https://docs.microsoft.com/en-us/windows/deployment/windows-autopilot/self-deploying`.

Something to bear in mind if you're utilizing hybrid Azure AD joins is that user-driven deployments will register the device to the on-premise Active Directory domain and Azure AD separately. Also, the hybrid method will require Intune Connector for Active Directory to be installed (Windows Server 2016, or later, is required) so that Intune can connect to the on-premises domain controller.

In-place upgrades

The recommended method for upgrading from Windows 7, or 8.1, to Windows 10 is doing an in-place upgrade, which uses the more traditional `setup.exe` experience of an OS installation. It migrates applications and files and requires less effort than a wipe-and-load scenario might entail.

You cannot upgrade a device from 32-bit to 64-bit, however, so you would need to select a different method such as wiping the device and performing a fresh installation if you run into this scenario.

You may use SCCM to perform the upgrade. After a configuration file is prepped, you'll need to create a task sequence where you specify the boot image and Windows 10 image package (which includes configuring BitLocker, the product key, and local admin account). On the System Preparation screen, select the package that includes the prepared Autopilot configuration file.

In the next section, we'll look at how you can determine Upgrade Readiness prior to moving existing devices to Windows 10.

Analyzing Upgrade Readiness for Windows 10

Upgrading to Windows 10 is arguably the easiest upgrade we've seen in recent memory:

- **Application compatibility**: 99% of Windows 7 apps will still run on Windows 10 (`https://www.microsoft.com/en-us/windowsforbusiness/simplified-updates`).
- **Device compatibility**: Any device running Windows 7 or later can run Windows 10. There is no need to buy new hardware.

That being said, you'll still want to do your homework to make sure your specific devices and applications are ready for the upgrade.

If you have an Azure subscription, you can use Windows Analytics (a set of Azure solutions) to analyze Upgrade Readiness, Update Compliance, and Device Health. To get started with Windows Analytics, follow these instructions to find each part of the workspace and link it to a new Azure Log Analytics workspace:

1. Go to the Azure portal at `https://portal.azure.com` and select **Create a resource**.
2. Search for `Upgrade Readiness`, select it, and then choose **Create**.
3. You'll be prompted to link to an existing (or create a new) Log Analytics workspace.
4. Select **Create**.

You'll repeat those steps twice more, replacing `Upgrade Readiness` with `Update Compliance` and then `Device Health`. Link the last two solutions to the same workspace you created in *step 3*.

 Windows Analytics' Upgrade Readiness solution will be retired on January 31, 2020 and Desktop Analytics will be available in its place. There will be a migration option available for eligible customers. Find more information at `https://support.microsoft.com/en-us/help/4521815/windows-analytics-retirement`.

We'll look at evaluating security features and deploying them in the next section.

Additional Windows 10 Enterprise security features

Let's review some additional topics and scenarios you might encounter in the exam that help you to improve your Windows 10 Enterprise security:

- **Identity and access management**:
    - Windows Hello for Business allows you to enable two-factor authentication with a biometric (such as facial recognition) or pin (specific to the device, not like a password that works across all devices and authenticates to a source of truth). If configuring Windows Hello for Business for **single sign-on** (**SSO**), devices will need to be added to Azure AD and enrolled in Intune first.

- **Threat protection**:
    - Microsoft Defender **Advanced Threat Protection** (**ATP**) reduces attack vulnerability and allows you to incorporate additional features alongside what you're already using from Microsoft Threat Protection (such as conditional access, Azure ATP, O365 ATP, and Cloud App Security).
    - Microsoft Defender ATP allows automated investigations and remediation of issues. The dashboard for automated investigations shows investigations of alerts from the past week by default and displays triggering alerts, the current investigation status, machines affected, investigation start date, and duration.
    - When devices are onboarded to Microsoft Defender ATP, you can choose where your data is stored (the United States versus Europe, for example). This location cannot be changed without offboarding devices and re-onboarding. You can read more about data storage privacy in Microsoft Defender ATP at `https://docs.microsoft.com/en-us/windows/security/threat-protection/microsoft-defender-atp/data-storage-privacy`.

- **Information protection**:
    - Use BitLocker to encrypt drives and reduce the risk of data loss from theft.

- Create **Windows Information Protection (WIP)** policies that encrypt data downloaded from SharePoint or shared drives when downloaded on a WIP-protected device, to prevent copying and pasting from corporate to personal apps. A WIP policy can also ensure that any data saved to removable media is encrypted. This means that, when an employee leaves, their key expires and the data is inaccessible from the removable media.

Summary

In this chapter we focused on the following exam topics:

- Planning for WaaS
- Planning the appropriate Windows 10 Enterprise deployment method
- Analyzing Upgrade Readiness for Windows 10
- Evaluating and deploying additional Windows 10 Enterprise security features

You have now learned how to use WaaS to manage and deploy regular OS updates to your organization's Windows 10 devices.

We used Windows Autopilot to automatically deploy Windows 10 with specified configurations to new devices and you can perform in-place upgrades on existing devices to preserve compatible apps and data.

We learned that, when devices are running earlier OSes, you can use Windows Analytics to help analyze the Upgrade Readiness of your devices to determine whether they're going to smoothly upgrade to Windows 10 or not. For example, you may determine there are applications that will not run on Windows 10, which may prompt you to ultimately decide not to perform an in-place upgrade until there is a suitable replacement solution for that application.

When planning your security feature configurations, you have many to choose from. We covered a handful of popular options in this chapter. Microsoft Defender ATP complements Microsoft Threat Protection by providing additional features such as conditional access and Azure security features. BitLocker helps to minimize data loss risk by encrypting drives in case devices are stolen or accessed by unauthorized individuals. And **Windows Information Protection (WIP)** policies protect data from copying and pasting or other user-managed functions that could place sensitive data types at risk.

In the next chapter you'll learn about implementing **Cloud App Security (CAS)**.

Questions

1. Your CIO asks for a report showing devices protected by Windows Defender ATP that had high-risk alerts in the last 7 days. What should you use?

   A. Azure Information Protection Dashboard
   B. Windows Defender ATP Automated Investigations
   C. Secure Store
   D. Security & Compliance Admin Center

2. You have 25 devices running Windows 8.1 and you need to upgrade to Windows 10 with minimal loss of data and installed applications. What should you do?

   A. Windows Autopilot Deployment
   B. Wipe and load the OS
   C. In-place upgrade
   D. MDM Enrollment

Further reading

- **Planning for Windows as a Service (WaaS)**:
    - *Overview of WaaS*: https://docs.microsoft.com/en-us/windows/deployment/update/waas-overview
- **Planning the appropriate Windows 10 Enterprise deployment method**:
    - *Windows 10 deployment considerations*: https://docs.microsoft.com/en-us/windows/deployment/planning/windows-10-deployment-considerations
- **Analyzing Upgrade Readiness for Windows 10**:
    - *Getting started with Upgrade Readiness*: https://docs.microsoft.com/en-us/windows/deployment/upgrade/upgrade-readiness-get-started
    - *Windows Analytics overview*: https://docs.microsoft.com/en-us/windows/deployment/update/windows-analytics-overview
- **Evaluating and deploying additional Windows 10 Enterprise security features**:
    - *Windows 10 Enterprise security*: https://docs.microsoft.com/en-us/windows/security/

Section 2: Microsoft 365 Security Threat Management

In this section, we will learn about Microsoft 365 Security Threat Management, which makes up 30-35% of the MS-101 exam. We'll focus on managing potential security threats and vulnerabilities and setting up **Advanced Threat Protection** (**ATP**).

This section includes the following chapters:

- Chapter 5, *Implementing Cloud App Security (CAS)*
- Chapter 6, *Implementing Threat Management*
- Chapter 7, *Implementing Windows Defender ATP*
- Chapter 8, *Managing Security Reports and Alerts*

5
Implementing Cloud App Security (CAS)

In this chapter, you'll learn how to manage potential security threats and vulnerabilities through utilizing **Cloud App Security** (**CAS**). CAS helps to identify and manage connected cloud apps such as G Suite and Box, set policies for conditional access based on specified criteria, and mitigate the risk of data loss by tracking anomalous behaviors and activities.

We'll be covering these specific exam topics in this chapter:

- Setting up CAS
- Configuring CAS policies
- Configuring connected apps
- Designing a CAS solution
- Managing CAS alerts
- Uploading CAS traffic logs

Let's start with the initial CAS setup.

Setting up CAS

Before you can begin using the CAS portal, you must first obtain a license for it (included in Enterprise Mobility + Security E5*) and whitelist this IP address: `104.42.231.28`. Whitelisting the IP address allows access to the portal.

 You can compare E3 and E5 EMS subscriptions and learn more about what is included at `https://www.microsoft.com/en-us/microsoft-365/enterprise-mobility-security/compare-plans-and-pricing`.

Once you've obtained a license and whitelisted the IP address, you'll need to implement the following steps to set up CAS:

1. Go to `portal.cloudappsecurity.com` and navigate to **Settings**, as shown in the following screenshot:

2. Configure the organization's display name (used in emails), the environment name (to help keep tenants clearly defined when performing administrative tasks), and your logo (150 x 150) for usage in messages and web pages generated by the service.

3. Configure your managed domains. This is arguably the most important aspect of the setup as it determines what to report and track, and who is considered an external user. Activities undertaken by external users aren't monitored, so be sure to include all of your company's managed domains for which you require reports and alerts. Click **Save**:

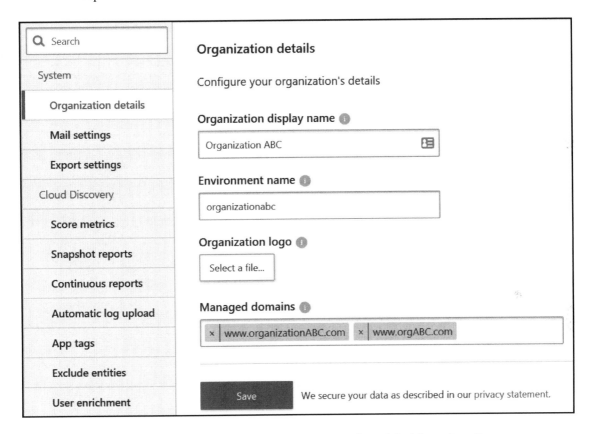

Once that's completed, you can look at integrating AIP for added functionality.

Integrating AIP with CAS

In order to integrate AIP with CAS, you'll need to first add the Office 365 (O365) app connector to allow monitoring O365 activity and files.

Once O365 has been added, and AIP has been enabled in the CAS settings, you'll be able to monitor O365 files with classification labels from AIP from within CAS, and assign labels manually or automatically via a policy. Perform the following to add the O365 app connector:

1. Under the **Investigate** fly-out menu, click **Add an app**:

2. Click the blue plus sign and select **Office 365**.

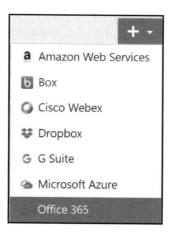

3. Click **Connect Office 365**.

4. Select the items you'd like to monitor and then click **Connect**:

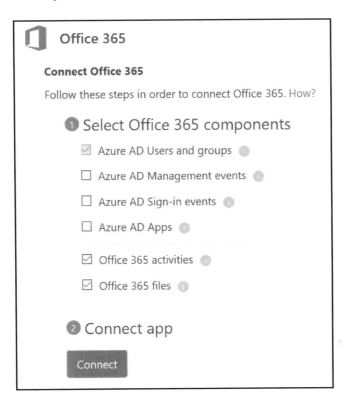

5. Now return to the CAS settings and navigate to **Settings** as shown in the following screenshot:

6. Select **Azure Information Protection** and check the box that lets you automatically scan new files for AIP classification labels, and then click **Save**:

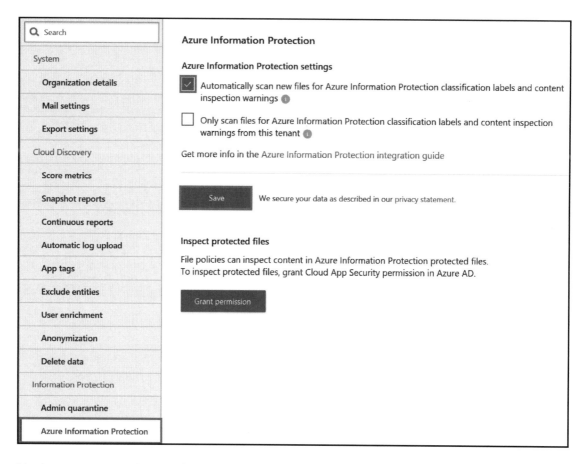

You've now set up CAS and integrated AIP. In the next section, we'll configure CAS policies.

Configuring CAS policies

You can create seven types of CAS policy from scratch, or start using a pre-defined template. To get started, go to CAS (`portal.cloudappsecurity.com`) and select either **Policies** or **Templates** from the **Control** fly-out menu:

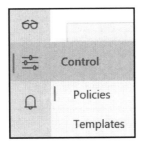

We'll look at policies first.

Policies

After selecting **Policies**, you'll notice that several already exist out of the box. You can modify these first if you wish, but at least review them so that you don't create a duplicate or conflicting policy.

If you're creating a policy from scratch, there are seven policy types to choose from:

The following table provides descriptions of the various policy types seen in the previous screenshot.

Policy type	Explanation
Access policy	Monitor login activity across cloud apps.
Activity policy	Monitor specific activities by users or large volumes of the same activity.
App discovery policy	Get notified when new apps are found in your company.
Cloud Discovery anomaly detection policy	Set up risk factors and get alerts when activities deviate from *the norm*.
File policy	Scan cloud apps for sensitive data or a risky shared status, and apply governance actions.
OAuth app policy	Discover apps authorized by many users, or those requesting high levels of permissions from users.
Session policy	Real-time monitoring and response to user activity.

Now, let's look at templates.

Templates

Currently, there are 35 templates available in the CAS portal. Rather than memorize them, just be aware of some of the important functions CAS provides for you by using templates, rather than setting up policies from scratch:

- New apps discovered with high usage
- The mass downloading of files in a short space of time
- Certain files shared with unauthorized domains
- Administrator activity from remote, unfamiliar locations
- Files shared with personal email addresses
- Files containing PHI, PCI, or PII identified in the cloud

Once you've selected a template to start from, you can customize it to your liking before saving it:

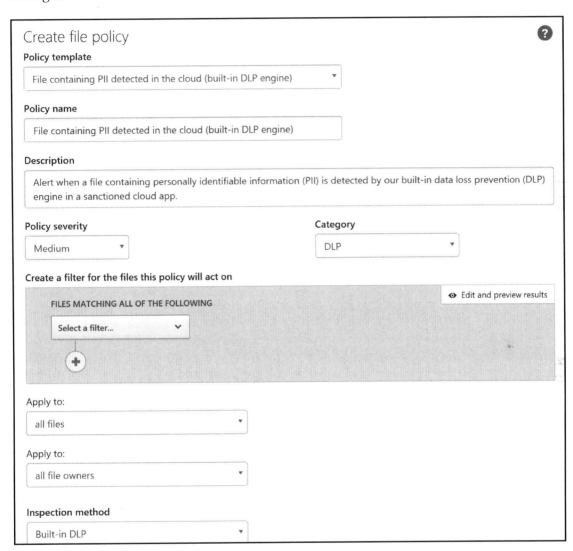

Create file policy   ?

Policy template

File containing PII detected in the cloud (built-in DLP engine)   ▼

Policy name

File containing PII detected in the cloud (built-in DLP engine)

Description

Alert when a file containing personally identifiable information (PII) is detected by our built-in data loss prevention (DLP) engine in a sanctioned cloud app.

Policy severity   **Category**

Medium   ▼   DLP   ▼

Create a filter for the files this policy will act on

                                                     👁 Edit and preview results

FILES MATCHING ALL OF THE FOLLOWING

Select a filter...   ∨

+

Apply to:

all files   ▼

Apply to:

all file owners   ▼

Inspection method

Built-in DLP   ▼

In the next section, we'll take a look at connecting other business apps, such as Google Drive for Business.

Configuring connected apps

Configuring connected apps allows you to monitor those apps you're connecting and to apply policies to them, as seen earlier in this chapter. The following steps detail how to configure connected apps.

1. From the CAS dashboard (`portal.cloudappsecurity.com`), expand **Investigate** and select **Connected apps**:

2. From your **Connected apps** dashboard, you can work with existing connected apps or add new ones by using the plus icon:

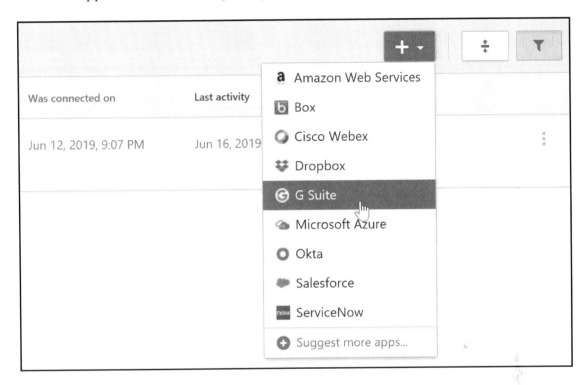

To be able to use CAS with certain apps, you'll need enterprise/business licenses and admin privileges to authorize CAS to scan the external services and perform remedial actions. For example, you'd need to be an admin of Dropbox Business/Enterprise to be able to connect and perform activities from CAS on your company's Dropbox environment. In addition, certain apps, such as G Suite, will require configuration of an API from their administration tools.

 Microsoft provides detailed and up-to-date instructions for configuring particular apps at `docs.microsoft.com`. Learn more at `https://docs.microsoft.com/en-us/cloud-app-security/enable-instant-visibility-protection-and-governance-actions-for-your-apps`, and check the left-hand navigation pane for quick links to specific apps.

The following section will explore the main differences between Microsoft CAS and Office 365 CAS.

Designing a CAS solution

The Microsoft world is full of acronyms and seemingly overlapping tools and services. When talking about CAS, it's wise to seek clarification when discussing licensing or functionality.

In CAS alone, there are **Microsoft Cloud App Security** (**MCAS**) and Office 365 **Cloud App Security** (**OCAS**). MCAS can connect to over 16,000 apps, while OCAS can only connect to about 750: basically, those that are Office 365 or similar in functionality. Another difference lies in deployment for discovery analysis. MCAS is the only option that allows automatic log uploading; OCAS provides only manual uploading.

If you intend to integrate with **Azure Information Protection** (**AIP**), you'll need to use MCAS.

 See a complete list of differences between MCAS and OCAS at `https://docs.microsoft.com/en-us/cloud-app-security/editions-cloud-app-security-o365`.

As far as licensing is concerned, all users who will be covered by CAS require a license for it. MCAS is included in Enterprise Mobility + Security E5. OCAS comes with Office 365 Enterprise E5.

Now, let's take a look at setting up CAS alerts.

Managing CAS alerts

Once you have policies in place, you can customize your alerts. Alerts can be viewed in the CAS portal (`portal.cloudappsecurity.com`) | **Alerts** (the lowest icon on the left):

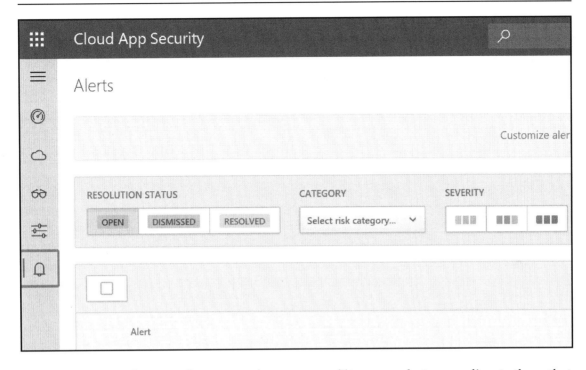

As can be seen in the preceding screenshot, you can filter your alerts according to those that are open, dismissed, or resolved. You can resolve alerts from this page as well. Other filters include the following:

- Resolution status
- Category (DLP and access control)
- Severity
- App (O365 or even more specific, such as just SharePoint-related alerts)
- Username
- Policy

Note that you can also choose to view these alerts in your O365 Security & Compliance center, but, at the time of writing, you're only able to view, and unable to resolve, alerts from Security & Compliance.

You can resolve alerts in a few different ways. In the case of those that are authorized violations or anomalies, you can dismiss the alerts. Anything questionable may require additional information from the user involved. Any serious or severe alerts may prompt you to force a user to change their password, or restrict file or app permissions.

As you're choosing an appropriate response to alerts, you can provide feedback to help improve your alerts. If an alert was accurate, but the activity was *legitimate*, you'd mark the alert as a **benign positive**, meaning it's of no concern. If an alert is *inaccurate*, you'd mark it as a **false positive**. A **true positive** is a legitimate alert, and you'd mark the alert as resolved once all remediation actions have been taken.

The following is globally a list of alerts you may encounter on your alert dashboard:

- Activity policy violation
- File policy violation
- Compromised account
- Inactive account
- New admin user
- New admin location
- New location
- New discovered service
- Suspicious activity
- Suspicious cloud use
- Use of personal account

For a full listing, examples, and potential remediation actions, check out the following link: `https://docs.microsoft.com/en-us/cloud-app-security/managing-alerts`.

Lastly in this chapter, we'll learn about upgrading network traffic logs to CAS for a more comprehensive monitoring solution.

Uploading CAS traffic logs

You can either manually upload network traffic logs (snapshots) or configure automatic log uploads. It's recommended you first upload a manual log to make sure it parses well before configuring automatic uploads.

First, we'll check out manual uploads, or snapshots.

Manual uploads

Manual uploads give you control of the upload process, but you are also more likely to cause gaps in data on account of human error or negligence. However, you may not need automatic uploads and you may just wish to analyze logs at specific times. To perform a manual upload, click **Create snapshot report** from the **Discover** tab of the CAS left navigation menu:

Once the dialog opens, you can configure the name and relevant data source for the report, and then upload up to 20 log files to be parsed:

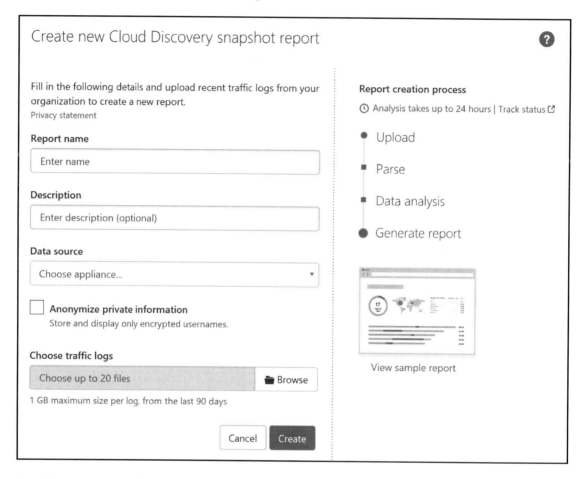

You'll receive a notification once the logs have been successfully analyzed and the resulting report is available for review. If you're wanting more continuous and reliable data, you'll want to configure automatic uploads, which we'll cover next.

Automatic uploads

As mentioned previously, one benefit of MCAS is the ability to automate the uploading of log files. You can use either **container** or **virtual appliance** (deprecated) as your deployment mode.

Container involves running a Docker image with Ubuntu or RHEL as your OS and can handle up to 50 GB per hour.

Virtual appliance uses Hyper-V, but since this is a deprecated and less flexible method, I'll use the container option for the following steps.

To begin setting up automatic uploading, we'll create a data source, and then a log collector in the CAS portal settings. It's recommended you create a data source for each network device to facilitate better monitoring and investigation. The following steps show how to create a data source and log collector:

1. Go to the CAS portal (`portal.cloudappsecurity.com`), navigate to Settings, and click **Log collectors**:

2. Select **Add data source...**, as shown in the following screenshot:

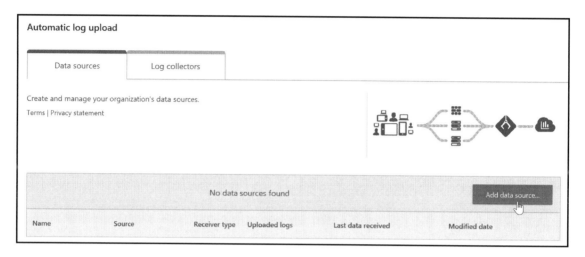

3. Name the data source and configure it for your specific setup. Then, click on **Add**:

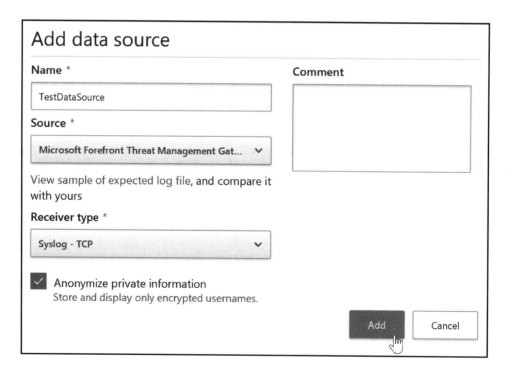

4. Select **Log collectors** | **Add log collector...**:

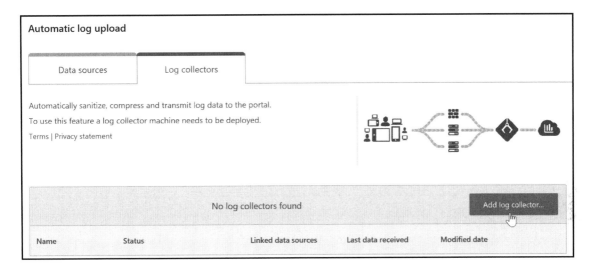

5. Your new data source will appear as an option. Configure the details for the machine you're using for collection and then save your work:

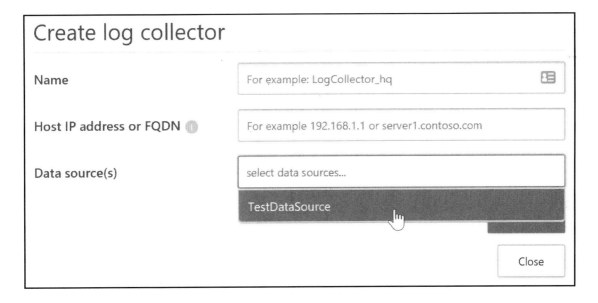

Next, you'll need to deploy your machine on site or in Azure. Depending on the OS, you'll follow varying steps, but they will generally all involve the following:

1. Download and install Docker.
2. Configure firewalls/proxies to export logs.
3. Verify your **Log collectors** dashboard in CAS shows that it's connected.

 Dive into specifics for each OS by selecting the appropriate article from the left-hand navigation bar at `https://docs.microsoft.com/en-us/cloud-app-security/discovery-docker`.

Summary

We have learned that CAS permits convenient the monitoring and mitigation of risky events and behaviors in your environment, such as irregular access or bulk activities. Because we can connect to, and monitor, many different apps and integrate with Azure ATP (as we'll see in the next chapter), CAS becomes our portal where everything comes together.

We also saw how CAS extends your data protection abilities by providing the option to protect other connected business apps, such as Dropbox or Google products, within your environment.

You learned that you can manage your alerts to make sure you're not over- or under-alerted once you begin to investigate and find root causes for certain alerts. You're also able to mark alerts as legitimate or not, which helps the system learn and report more effectively in the future.

You can manually or automatically upload network traffic logs to CAS and monitor that additional data from a single dashboard alongside your other CAS alerts.

In the following chapter, we'll discuss the implementation of threat management.

Questions

1. You've added G Suite as a connected app to the CAS **Connected apps** dashboard. You get no data within 24 hours, however. Which of the following could be the cause?

   A. G Suite not configured properly
   B. Insufficient permissions used to authenticate to G Suite
   C. Advanced Threat Protection not configured properly
   D. The Security & Compliance center is blocking the connection

2. Number the following steps in the correct order to configure automatic uploads of log files in Microsoft Cloud App Security.

   ___A. Add a log collector in CAS
   ___B. Download and install Docker on the collection machine
   ___C. Add a data source in CAS
   ___D. Configure firewalls/proxies and ensure that the log collector status is *connected* on CAS

Further reading

- **Setting up Cloud App Security (CAS)**:
  - *Basic setup for Cloud App Security*: https://docs.microsoft.com/en-us/cloud-app-security/general-setup
  - *Microsoft Cloud App Security*: https://docs.microsoft.com/en-us/cloud-app-security/

- **Configuring Cloud App Security (CAS) policies**:
  - *Control cloud apps with policies*: https://docs.microsoft.com/en-us/cloud-app-security/control-cloud-apps-with-policies
  - *Protect apps with Microsoft Cloud App Security Conditional Access App Control*: https://docs.microsoft.com/en-us/cloud-app-security/proxy-intro-aad

- **Configuring connected apps**:
  - *Connect apps*: https://docs.microsoft.com/en-us/cloud-app-security/enable-instant-visibility-protection-and-governance-actions-for-your-apps

- **Designing a Cloud App Security (CAS) solution**:
    - *Quickstart: Get started with Microsoft Cloud App Security*: `https://docs.microsoft.com/en-us/cloud-app-security/getting-started-with-cloud-app-security`
    - *What are the differences between Microsoft Cloud App Security and Office 365 Cloud App Security?*: `https://docs.microsoft.com/en-us/cloud-app-security/editions-cloud-app-security-o365`

- **Managing Cloud App Security (CAS) alerts**:
    - *Manage alerts*: `https://docs.microsoft.com/en-us/cloud-app-security/managing-alerts`

- **Uploading Cloud App Security (CAS) traffic logs**:
    - *Configure automatic log uploads for continuous reports*: `https://docs.microsoft.com/en-us/cloud-app-security/discovery-docker`

6
Implementing Threat Management

Understanding the **Advanced Threat Protection** (**ATP**) capabilities of Azure and Office 365 will help you better plan your organization's strategy for proactively designing and managing an ATP solution and its policies.

In this chapter, we'll be covering the following exam topics:

- Planning a threat management solution
- Designing and configuring Azure ATP policies
- Designing and configuring Microsoft 365 ATP policies
- Monitoring **Advanced Threat Analytics** (**ATA**) incidents

Let's start with planning a threat management solution and understanding the options available to you within your subscriptions.

Planning a threat management solution

One of the nice things about Office 365 subscriptions is that all of them come with *some* level of threat protection. Certain subscriptions and add-ons give you advanced features:

- **Exchange Online Protection (EOP)**: Cloud-based email filtering for both on-premises and cloud-hosted mailboxes.
  - Anti-malware protection
  - Anti-phishing protection
  - Anti-spam protection
  - Zero-hour auto purge (post-delivery threat remediation)

- **Exchange Online**: Two plans available, with Plan 2 including **data loss prevention (DLP)**
  - Audit logging
- **Azure Advanced Threat Protection (ATP)**: Included in Enterprise Mobility + Security E5 or as standalone
  - Monitor and remediate threats on-prem and in the cloud
  - Protect identities
  - Flag behavioral anomalies
- **Microsoft 365 ATP**: Included in E5 licenses or as standalone
  - Office 365 ATP Plan 1:
    - Time-of-click malicious link/file protection in email and Office files:
      - ATP Safe Attachments policies
      - ATP Safe Links policies
    - Advanced anti-phishing protection
  - Office 365 ATP Plan 2:
    - All of Office 365 ATP Plan 1
    - Attack simulator
    - Automated investigations and response
    - Threat explorer
    - Threat investigation and response
    - Threat trackers

All of the above are powerful options for designing a comprehensive threat management solution. Depending on your unique environment, some services or apps may be more suitable than others and some may be unnecessary. In the sections that follow, we'll explore some of the mentioned solutions further.

Next, let's look at designing and configuring Azure ATP.

Designing and configuring Azure ATP

Azure ATP is cloud-based but involves installing sensors on-prem to help manage risks in both locations and more comprehensively protect users. It involves the following:

- Learning-based analytics and suspicious behavior identification
- Protecting AD credentials

- Reducing attack surfaces
- Fast and clear incident reporting

Before you can use Azure ATP, you'll need to create and configure your Azure ATP instance. These are the basic steps. You would repeat these steps for each unique AD forest:

1. Create an instance in the Azure ATP portal.
2. Provide local Active Directory forest credentials.
3. Download a sensor setup.
4. Install a sensor on a dedicated server or a domain controller.
5. Configure the sensor.

It's recommended to install one sensor per Active Directory forest. The following screenshot shows how you're able to provide multiple sets of credentials for untrusted forests in the **Directory services** section:

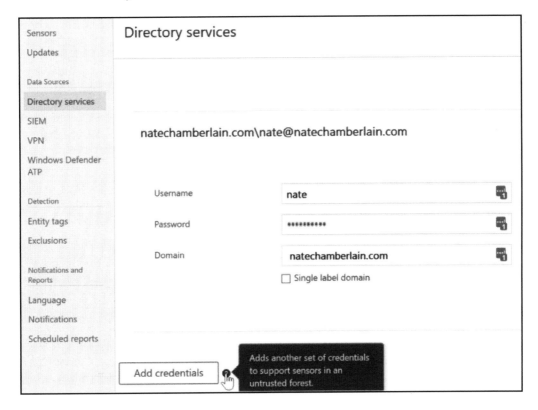

Let's walk through setting up a sensor.

Setting up a sensor

The following are detailed steps for setting up your first sensor in a single-forest environment:

1. Go to `portal.atp.azure.com` and click **Create**:

2. Follow the steps outlined in the wizard to connect to Active Directory, and install your first sensor on a **domain controller** (**DC**) or on its own dedicated server:

If installing on a dedicated server, the sensor uses **port mirroring** and is called an **Azure ATP standalone sensor**. If installing on a DC, it's just an **Azure ATP sensor**.

3. Creating the instance will automatically create three cloud security groups (administrators, users, and viewers) associated with it in your Azure AD. You can access and edit these from Azure ATP by selecting **Manage role groups** from the left-hand navigation menu. Learn more about the specific permissions granted by default for these groups at `https://docs.microsoft.com/en-us/azure-advanced-threat-protection/atp-role-groups`.

4. Download and extract the contents of the sensor setup ZIP from the server to which it will belong. Run the setup file and be ready to paste the access key generated on the download step of the wizard:

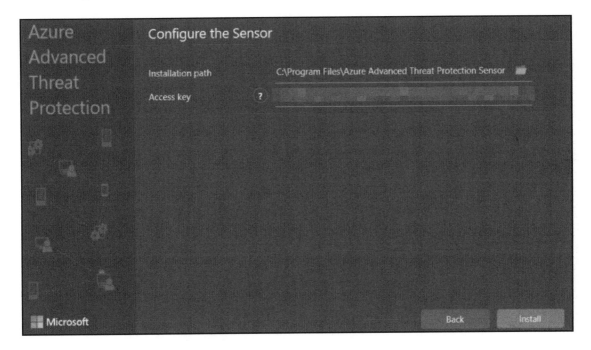

5. Back in the Azure ATP portal, you can now verify that the sensor is running and configure any additional settings, such as a unique description for the sensor.

In the following section, we'll design and configure Microsoft 365 ATP policies.

Designing and configuring Microsoft 365 ATP policies

You have several options available to you to protect your users from incoming malicious threats. Phishing attacks, malicious attachments and links, and even dangerous uploads within your office apps can be prevented by taking the time to configure ATP policies. There are four types of policies you'll want to take a look at when designing your Office 365 ATP policies:

- ATP Safe Attachments
- ATP Safe Links
- ATP for SharePoint, OneDrive, and Microsoft Teams
- ATP anti-phishing protection

We'll explore each of these in the following sub-sections.

ATP Safe Attachments

Safe Attachments checks all incoming messages and attachments for malicious content by looking for virus/malware signatures. If nothing is detected, the message continues to its destination:

1. Go to `protection.office.com`.
2. Click on **Threat management** | **Policy** | **ATP safe attachments**:

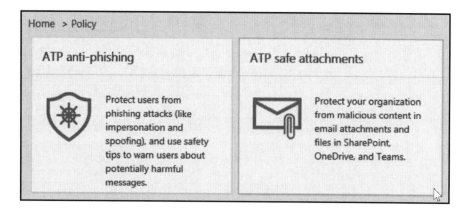

3. Click the + sign to add a new policy:

4. Configure the settings as appropriate and save. As seen in the screenshot that follows, you have the option of monitoring, blocking, replacing, or dynamically delivering attachments:

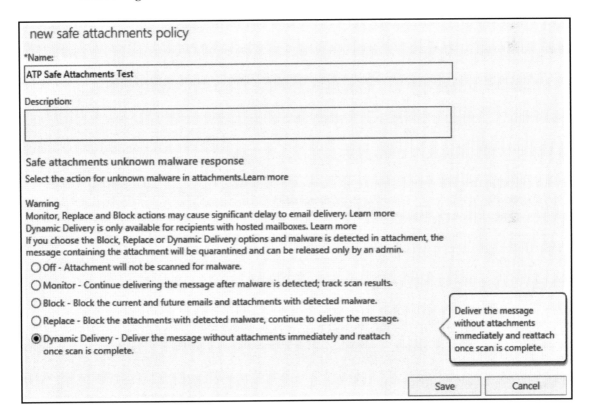

To review your options in the previous screenshot, you can respond to malware by configuring the policy's response as follows:

1. **Off**: Attachments aren't scanned.
2. **Monitor**: Deliver the message after malware detection and track the scan results.
3. **Block**: Block the email and future emails with detected malware.
4. **Replace**: Block the attachments with malware, but deliver the message.
5. **Dynamic delivery**: Deliver the message without the attachment until the scan is complete, and then reattach it.

Next, we'll cover ATP Safe Links.

ATP Safe Links

Safe Links block malicious links and provide time-of-click analysis for all other links:

1. Go to `protection.office.com`.
2. Click on **Threat management** | **Policy** | **ATP Safe Links**:

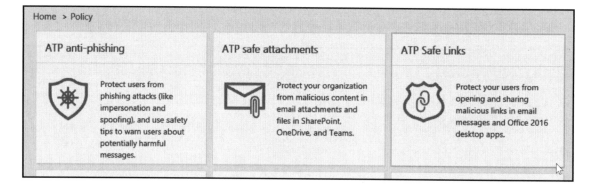

3. You're able to create and configure policies that apply to the entire organization or just specific groups:

   1. **Policies that apply to the entire organization**: As seen in the following screenshot, you can block specific URLs. You can use safe links in Office 365 ProPlus and Office for iOS and Android. It is recommended that you check all the boxes under **Settings that apply to content except email**:

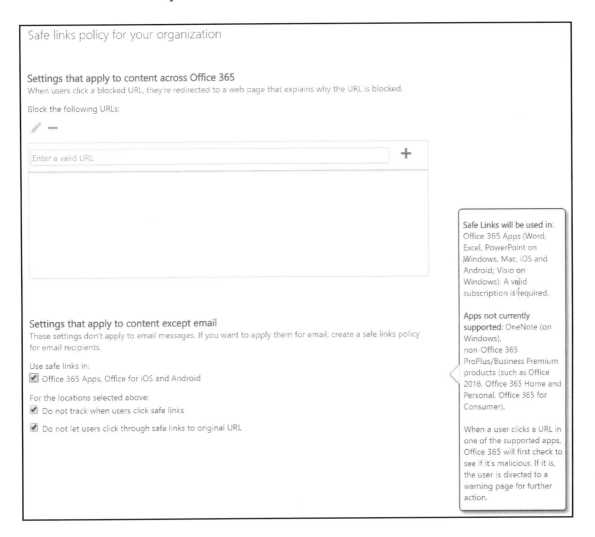

Safe links policy for your organization

Settings that apply to content across Office 365
When users click a blocked URL, they're redirected to a web page that explains why the URL is blocked.

Block the following URLs:

Enter a valid URL   +

Safe Links will be used in: Office 365 Apps (Word, Excel, PowerPoint on Windows, Mac, iOS and Android; Visio on Windows). A valid subscription is required.

Apps not currently supported: OneNote (on Windows), non-Office 365 ProPlus/Business Premium products (such as Office 2016, Office 365 Home and Personal, Office 365 for Consumer).

When a user clicks a URL in one of the supported apps, Office 365 will first check to see if it's malicious. If it is, the user is directed to a warning page for further action.

Settings that apply to content except email
These settings don't apply to email messages. If you want to apply them for email, create a safe links policy for email recipients.

Use safe links in:
☑ Office 365 Apps, Office for iOS and Android

For the locations selected above:
☑ Do not track when users click safe links

☑ Do not let users click through safe links to original URL

2. **Policies that apply to specific recipients**: Here, you can get granular on settings for specific groups, perhaps being more restrictive for higher-risk individuals such as those regularly handling sensitive information. You will assign the policy after you configure its available options seen here:

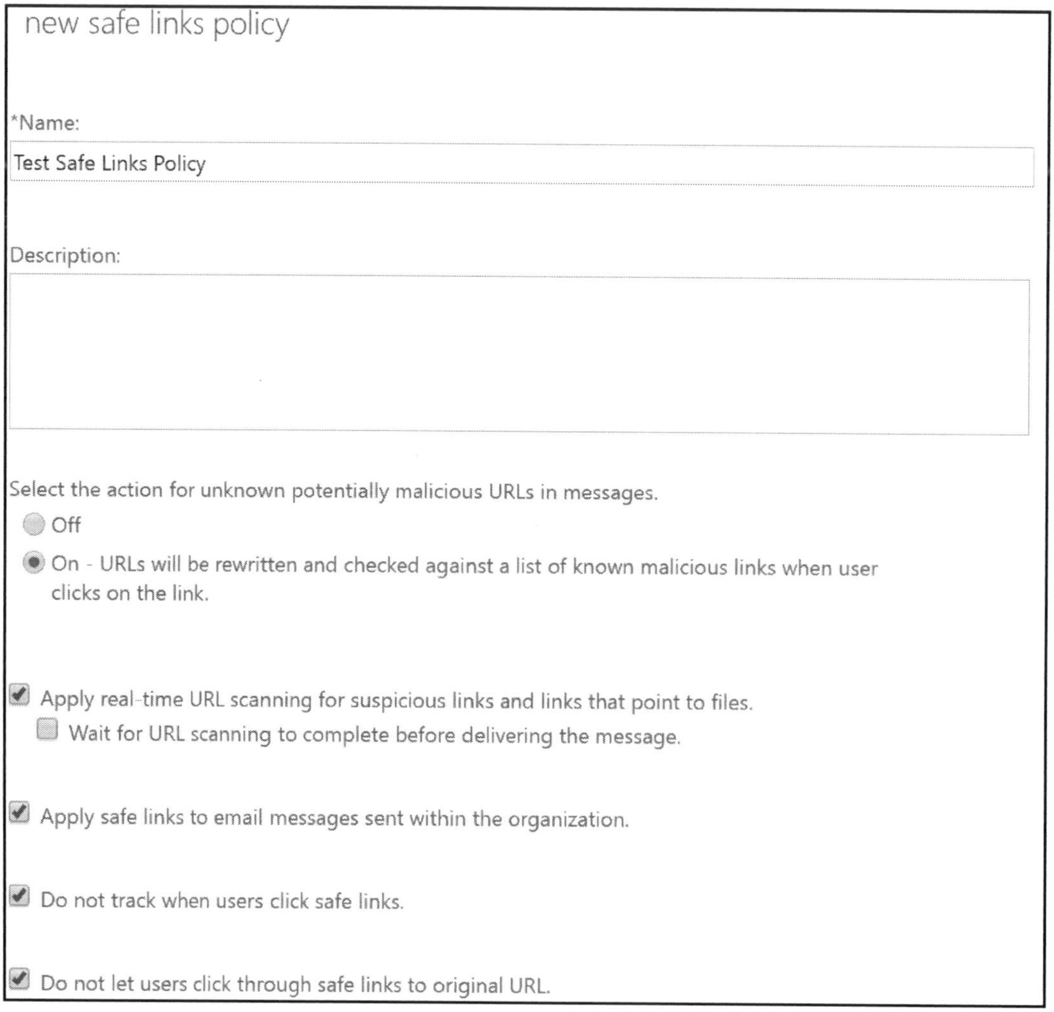

---

new safe links policy

*Name:

Test Safe Links Policy

Description:

Select the action for unknown potentially malicious URLs in messages.
- ○ Off
- ● On - URLs will be rewritten and checked against a list of known malicious links when user clicks on the link.

- ☑ Apply real-time URL scanning for suspicious links and links that point to files.
  - ☐ Wait for URL scanning to complete before delivering the message.

- ☑ Apply safe links to email messages sent within the organization.

- ☑ Do not track when users click safe links.

- ☑ Do not let users click through safe links to original URL.

If you select **On** for rewriting URLs, you'll be able to check **Use safe attachments to scan downloadable content**, which allows you to detect when a link goes directly to a file download. Safe Links then utilizes Safe Attachments to scan the file content prior to download.

Now we'll look at ATP for collaboration apps in Office 365.

ATP for SharePoint, OneDrive, and Microsoft Teams

Office 365 collaboration tools are scanned for malicious content being shared, blocking content when appropriate. These can be configured in the ATP Safe Attachments policies mentioned previously.

On the **Safe attachments** settings configuration page, just check the box for **Turn on ATP for SharePoint, OneDrive, and Microsoft Teams**:

Home > Safe attachments

Safe attachments

Use this page to protect your organization from malicious content in email attachments and files in SharePoint, OneDrive, and Microsoft Teams.

Protect files in SharePoint, OneDrive, and Microsoft Teams
If a file in any SharePoint, OneDrive, or Microsoft Teams library is identified as malicious, ATP will prevent users from opening and downloading the file. Learn more about ATP for SharePoint, OneDrive, and Microsoft Teams

☑ Turn on ATP for SharePoint, OneDrive, and Microsoft Teams

The last thing we'll look at in this section are ATP anti-phishing protection features.

ATP anti-phishing protection

Anti-phishing provides protection from emails attempting to impersonate a user or account from your domain. Note that, by default, you already have several ATP policies active. Review/edit those as needed before creating new policies that could duplicate or conflict.

- Impersonation (user or domain)
- Spoof (move messages to junk)
- Advanced settings (what's your tolerance threshold?)

Notice, in the following screenshot, how we are able to configure users and specific domains the policy applies to, which actions to take for impersonation and spoofing attempts, when and where to display safety tips, and much more:

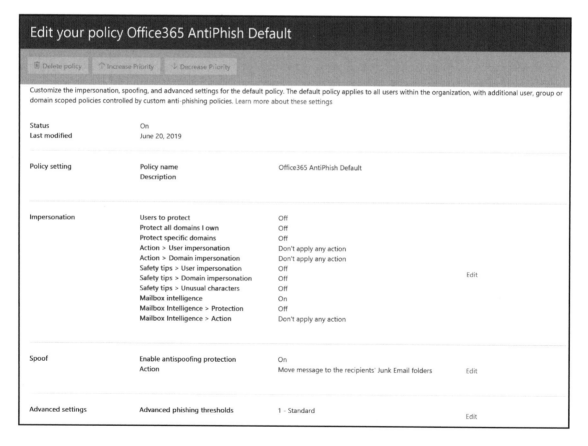

Edit your policy Office365 AntiPhish Default

Delete policy   ↑ Increase Priority   ↓ Decrease Priority

Customize the impersonation, spoofing, and advanced settings for the default policy. The default policy applies to all users within the organization, with additional user, group or domain scoped policies controlled by custom anti-phishing policies. Learn more about these settings

Status	On	
Last modified	June 20, 2019	
Policy setting	Policy name	Office365 AntiPhish Default
	Description	
Impersonation	Users to protect	Off
	Protect all domains I own	Off
	Protect specific domains	Off
	Action > User impersonation	Don't apply any action
	Action > Domain impersonation	Don't apply any action
	Safety tips > User impersonation	Off
	Safety tips > Domain impersonation	Off	Edit
	Safety tips > Unusual characters	Off
	Mailbox intelligence	On
	Mailbox Intelligence > Protection	Off
	Mailbox Intelligence > Action	Don't apply any action
Spoof	Enable antispoofing protection	On
	Action	Move message to the recipients' Junk Email folders	Edit
Advanced settings	Advanced phishing thresholds	1 - Standard	Edit

When you're ready to create additional policies beyond what's available by default, follow these steps:

1. Go to `protection.office.com`.
2. Click on **Threat management** | **Policy** | **ATP anti-phishing**:

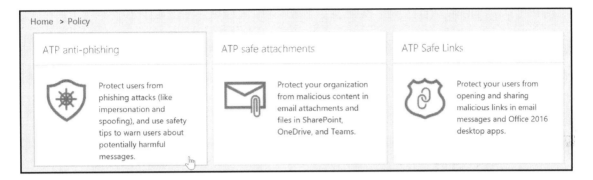

3. Click **+Create** and name your anti-phishing policy. Click **Next**:

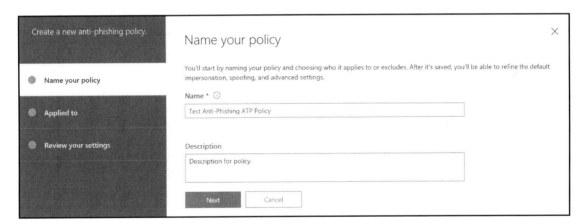

4. Choose conditions under which the policy will apply. These conditions begin with **Applied if...** or **Except when...** You can have multiple conditions if you wish, but select them one at a time:

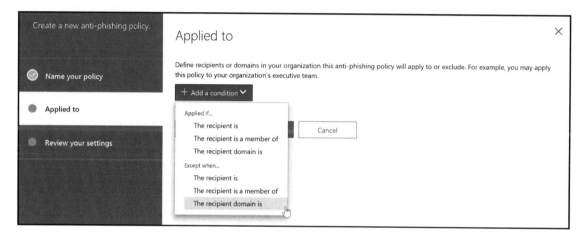

5. When you've finished designing all conditions, click **Next**:

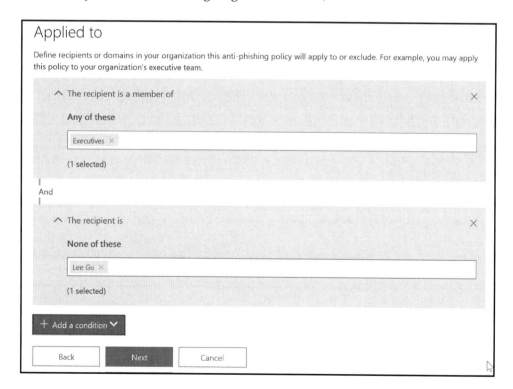

6. Confirm that all of the details look correct, and click **Create this policy**:

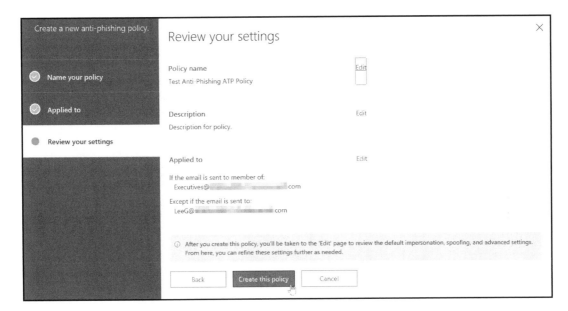

7. You'll now be taken to an edit page for the policy, where you can refine settings/actions. One of these is mailbox intelligence, which helps prevent false positives when it comes to detecting impersonation attempts:

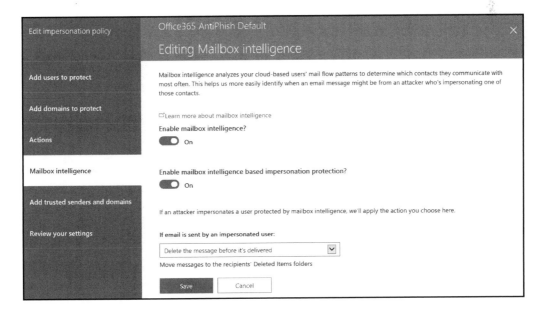

In the last section of this chapter, let's look at monitoring ATA incidents.

Monitoring ATA incidents

ATA resides on-premises and protects you from internal threats and cyber attacks. You can deploy it by using port mirroring from your domain controllers to the ATA gateway (on its own server) or by deploying a **lightweight gateway** (**LGW**) directly on the domain controllers.

ATA can detect anomalous logins, password sharing, sensitive group changes, malicious attacks from known attack types, weak protocols, and more.

One type of attack that you may see in the exam is a **pass-the-hash attack**, in which the attacker uses the underlying hash behind an account's password to authenticate to computers, rather than needing the plain-text password itself. You might suspect this if you were alerted to a user authenticating to machines they wouldn't normally (anomalous behavior). To remediate this, you'd change the user's password, but any Kerberos tickets created by the attacker while the account was compromised would still be valid. To invalidate all tickets in the domain, you'd have to reset the standard KRBTGT account's password twice.

There are a significant number of attack types, more than would fit within the scope and purpose of this chapter. However, if you wish to explore more attack types and remediation tactics, you can review the documentation at `https://docs.microsoft.com/en-us/advanced-threat-analytics/suspicious-activity-guide`.

ATA consists of the single **ATA Center**, which receives data from the **ATA Gateway(s)** (lightweight on a domain controller, or standalone). You can deploy both lightweight and standalone gateways.

The ATA Console provides the following reports on a regular basis via scheduled emails or on-demand as needed:

- Summary report
- Modification of sensitive groups (such as administrators)
- Passwords exposed in plain text
- Lateral movement paths to sensitive accounts (from non-sensitive accounts)

The ATA Console's landing page is an attack timeline that lists suspicious activity detected chronologically. For each activity, you can choose to do the following:

- Close (mark resolved; will trigger again if found)
- Suppress (suppress this alert and similar alerts for now, but will fire again for new instances or after a period of time)
- Delete (deletes alert; unrecoverable)
- Exclude (mark as safe; for expected issues due to setup)

When working with alerts, you may refer to them as true or false positives or a benign true positive.

- **True positives** are real, malicious events.
- **Benign true positives** are rightfully triggered as an alert but are not malicious in nature (these would include tests).
- **False positives** are alerts that shouldn't have triggered but did.

Read more about ATA issue remediation
at `https://docs.microsoft.com/en-us/advanced-threat-analytics/what-is-ata`.

Summary

This chapter introduced us to a deeper level of threat management possibilities in Microsoft 365. We covered the following exam topics:

- Planning a threat management solution
- Designing and configuring Azure ATP policies
- Designing and configuring Microsoft 365 ATP policies
- Monitoring ATA incidents

Many of the advanced threat management services can be purchased standalone, or are included in subscription packages such as Enterprise Mobility + Security E5.

Azure ATP sensors are installed one per AD forest and help protect your identities and mitigate suspicious activity threats on-prem or in the cloud.

Microsoft 365 ATP policies will likely appear in the exam multiple times, testing your ability to identify the correct tool/policy to use in different scenarios. Let's review the main options:

- ATP Safe Attachments protects users from potentially malicious attachment content in emails.
- ATP Safe Links replaces URLs in emails with safe URLs and can protect users from clicking on or sharing something malicious.
- ATP for SharePoint, OneDrive, and Microsoft Teams is configured from *within* the ATP Safe Attachments configuration screen. This protects users from opening potentially malicious content within each app.
- ATP anti-phishing protection protects users from impersonation attempts.

ATA incidents are events classified as malicious or risky activity that could require investigation or mitigative actions by an administrator. You can also set up alerts for certain types of sensitive events such as administrator role group modification.

In the next chapter, we'll look at implementing Windows Defender ATP.

Questions

1. Using the default **anti-phishing** policy that follows, what will happen when domain impersonation is detected?

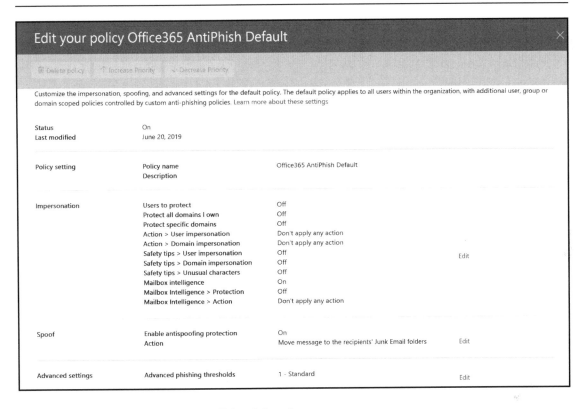

A. The message will be deleted.
B. The message will be moved to the junk email folder.
C. Nothing.
D. The message will be moved to quarantine.

2. **Requirement**: You need to make sure links in email messages that directly download documents are re-written and the file is scanned for malicious content.

    Action: You configure an ATP Safe Attachments policy.
    Does this satisfy the requirement?
    A. Yes
    B. No

Further reading

- **Plan a threat management solution**:
    - *Protect against threats in Office 365*: https://docs.microsoft.com/en-us/Office365/SecurityCompliance/protect-against-threats

- **Design and configure Azure ATP policies**:
    - *What is Azure Advanced Threat Protection?*: https://docs.microsoft.com/en-us/azure-advanced-threat-protection/what-is-atp
    - *Quickstart: Create your Azure ATP instance*: https://docs.microsoft.com/en-us/azure-advanced-threat-protection/install-atp-step1
    - *Quickstart: Configure Azure ATP sensor settings*: https://docs.microsoft.com/en-us/azure-advanced-threat-protection/install-atp-step5

- **Design and Configure Microsoft 365 ATP policies**:
    - *Office 365 Advanced Threat Protection Service Description*: https://docs.microsoft.com/en-us/office365/servicedescriptions/office-365-advanced-threat-protection-service-description#advanced-threat-protection-atp-capabilities
    - *Set up Office 365 ATP Safe Links policies*: https://docs.microsoft.com/en-us/microsoft-365/security/office-365-security/set-up-atp-safe-links-policies
    - *Set up Office 365 ATP Safe Attachments policies*: https://docs.microsoft.com/en-us/microsoft-365/security/office-365-security/set-up-atp-safe-attachments-policies

- **Monitor Advanced Threat Analytics (ATA) incidents**:
    - *What is Advanced Threat Analytics?*: https://docs.microsoft.com/en-us/advanced-threat-analytics/what-is-ata
    - *Advanced Threat Analytics suspicious activity guide*: https://docs.microsoft.com/en-us/advanced-threat-analytics/suspicious-activity-guide
    - *Working with Suspicious Activities*: https://docs.microsoft.com/en-us/advanced-threat-analytics/working-with-suspicious-activities

7
Implementing Windows Defender ATP

In addition to Azure and Office 365 ATP, Microsoft Defender **Advanced Threat Protection** (**ATP**) offers even more settings and policies, which makes sense in certain scenarios when we're dealing with Windows 10 and Mac devices. In this chapter, we will learn about the requirements and best use cases for Microsoft Defender ATP.

In this chapter, we will cover the following exam objectives:

- Planning our Windows Defender ATP solution
- Configuring our preferences
- Implementing Windows Defender ATP policies
- Enabling and configuring the security features of Windows 10 Enterprise

 At the time of writing this book, the exam requirements still list Windows Defender ATP as a topic. However, Microsoft is in the process of updating the documentation and branding to make it Microsoft Defender ATP since it's now available for macOS. In this chapter, we'll refer to it as Microsoft Defender ATP since that's mostly what you'll find in the relevant documentation and your environments. But if you see Windows Defender ATP somewhere (for example, we'll leave the exam requirements as they're listed on the exam site), remember that it's the same thing being used interchangeably.

In the upcoming sections, we'll cover everything you'll need in order to plan for and deploy Microsoft Defender ATP to improve the security of your environment and its devices. Let's begin by planning our Microsoft Defender ATP solution.

Planning our Windows Defender ATP solution

Microsoft Defender ATP, formerly known as Windows Defender ATP, is a hub of information about your environment that's collected from endpoints embedded in Windows 10. It incorporates threat intelligence and machine learning to identify and remediate issues, making sure you're protected against the latest threats. Its features, many of which we'll cover throughout each section in this chapter, include the following:

- Threat and vulnerability management
- Attack surface reduction
- Next-generation protection
- Endpoint detection and response
- Automated investigation and remediation
- Secure score
- Microsoft threat experts
- Management and APIs
- Microsoft Threat Protection

To be able to use Microsoft Defender ATP, you must have an E5 license, your hardware must be running Windows 7 or later, and Windows Server must be 2008 R2 or later. It is essential to use Microsoft Defender ATP when using Defender as your Windows protection solution and when moving to the modern management of Windows 10.

An important feature in the portal (`securitycenter.windows.com`) is the ability to run reports on the machines you're monitoring. This allows you to create and add tags that help to filter and assign machine group membership. For example, you may create an admin group of machines that allows you to configure different threat remediation tactics or sensitivity levels, or run a report just for those admin machines. So, while planning, consider how you can organize machines in your environment.

When setting up machine group criteria, note that **machines will only be added to the highest-ranking group they're matched to**. This is to reference: `https://docs.microsoft.com/en-us/windows/security/threat-protection/microsoft-defender-atp/machine-groups`.

In the next section, we'll configure the preferences for Microsoft Defender ATP.

Configuring our preferences

Later, we'll cover reducing your attack surface (all of the possible vulnerabilities in your environment) and next-generation protection with Microsoft Defender, but first, we'll take a look at two topics you'll want to be aware of for the exam:

- Secure score dashboard security controls
- Microsoft Threat Experts capabilities

Secure score dashboard security controls

Secure score dashboard security controls include and measure the following metrics. I've paraphrased these from `https://docs.microsoft.com/en-us/windows/security/threat-protection/microsoft-defender-atp/secure-score-dashboard`, where you can also view the remediation steps for each:

- Endpoint Detection and Response (EDR):
    - The Microsoft Defender ATP sensor is on and communication is not impaired.
    - Data collection is working correctly.
- Windows Defender Antivirus (AV):
    - Windows Defender AV is on and reporting correctly.
    - Security intelligence is updated.
    - Real-time protection is on.
    - Potentially Unwanted Application (PUA) protection is enabled.
- Operating system updates:
    - Sensors are healthy and configured appropriately.
    - The latest security updates are installed.
- Windows Defender Exploit Guard (EG):
    - System-level protection settings, attack surface reduction rules, and controlled folder access settings are configured correctly.
- Windows Defender Application Guard (AG):
    - Hardware/software prerequisites are met.
    - Windows Defender AG is turned on for compatible machines.
    - Managed mode is on.

- Windows Defender SmartScreen:
    - All settings (apps/files, Edge, and store apps) are at least set to **Warn**. It could also be set to **Block** or, for store apps, **Off**.
- Windows Defender Firewall:
    - Windows Defender Firewall is turned on for all network connections.
    - Secure domain, private, and public profiles by setting inbound connections to **Blocked**.
- BitLocker:
    - Drives are supported and encrypted.
    - Any suspended protection is resumed.
- Windows Defender Credential Guard:
    - Hardware/software prerequisites met.
    - Turned on for compatible machines.

Microsoft Threat Experts capabilities

You can apply for Microsoft Threat Experts (`securitycenter.windows.com` | **Settings** | **General** | **Advanced features** | **Microsoft Threat Experts**) to gain access to its tools. Once approved, you can toggle it on and off from the same location.

Once you've enabled Microsoft Threat Experts, you can get alerts emailed to you or view alerts on the Microsoft Defender ATP portal dashboard.

 You can find out more about Microsoft Threat Experts at `https://docs.microsoft.com/en-us/windows/security/threat-protection/microsoft-defender-atp/configure-microsoft-threat-experts`.

Implementing Windows Defender ATP policies

To enforce conditional access policies, you'll need to set up a device compliance policy that checks your devices' threat level in Microsoft Defender ATP. Azure AD registered devices are not eligible for conditional access unless they are enrolled in Intune. That being said, take note of the following requirements for conditional access with Microsoft Defender ATP:

- You must have an Enterprise Mobility and Security E5 license or Microsoft 365 Enterprise E5 license.
- You must have Intune configured with Windows 10 devices joined to Azure AD.
- You must have Microsoft Defender ATP and the portal (Security Center).

Assuming you have met these requirements, you can enable conditional access by following these steps:

1. Go to Microsoft Defender Security Center (securitycenter.windows.com).
2. Turn on the Microsoft Intune connection (advanced features).
3. Turn on Microsoft Defender ATP integration in Intune. Before you can continue, Intune will provide instructions for doing this as seen in the following screenshot:

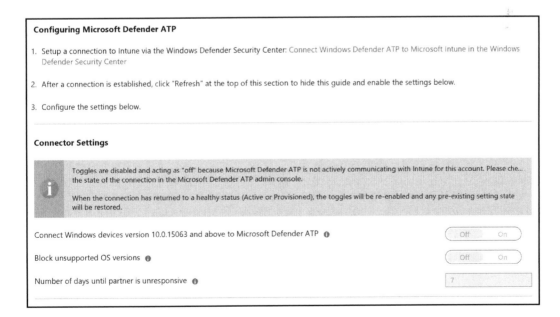

You must have completed *step 2* before you're able to configure Microsoft Defender ATP. If you forget, Intune won't allow you to turn on Microsoft Defender ATP until you've configured it. Only after doing this, will you be able to complete the steps that follow.

4. Create and assign the compliance policy in Intune. Set it so that the device must be at or under a specified threat level (see `Chapter 2`, *Managing Device Compliance*).

5. Create an Azure AD Conditional Access policy, restricting access to compliant devices (see `Chapter 2`, *Managing Device Compliance*).

Finally, let's enable and configure any of the features that will reduce our attack surface and provide next-generation protection.

Enabling and configuring the security features of Windows 10 Enterprise

In this final section of this chapter, we'll cover two ways you can enable and configure security features in Windows 10 Enterprise:

- Attack surface reduction
- Next-generation protection

Reducing your attack surface can be done in many ways, and we'll go into detail on a few of those ways here. Next-generation protection helps to make sure you're up to date at all times and benefitting from the security knowledge that you've gained and incorporated from Microsoft in near-real-time.

Let's start by looking at reducing our attack surface.

Attack surface reduction

Most of the following methods of reducing the attack surface in your environment can be configured in a number of ways, including via Intune, **System Center Configuration Manager (SCCM)**, group policy, the Windows Security app, Windows features settings, **Windows Management Instrumentation (WMI)**, and PowerShell.

We'll cover the following tactics of reducing your attack surface:

- Install application guard
- Enable application control
- Exploit protection
- Network protection
- Controlled folder access
- Network firewall

Install application guard

Application guard is a Windows feature that will check entered URLs against a whitelist to determine whether an employee is allowed to access it through their browser. If not, they can either be blocked or the URL can be opened in a Hyper-V-enabled container to protect the host machine. To use this feature, simply enable it by using any of the methods that we mentioned at the start of this section:

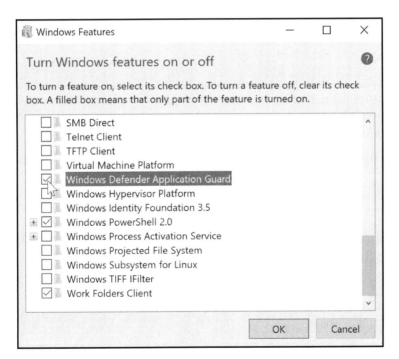

Once enabled, you can configure settings such as disallowing copy/paste or downloads from any URLs that are opened in the Hyper-V-enabled container.

You can read more about the configurable settings for Application Guard at `https://docs.microsoft.com/en-us/windows/security/threat-protection/windows-defender-application-guard/configure-wd-app-guard`.

Enable application control

Application control is primarily managed via PowerShell and allows you to control the applications, as well as plugins, that are allowed to run in your organization's device groups.

 You can read more about Microsoft Defender Application Control at `https://docs.microsoft.com/en-us/windows/security/threat-protection/windows-defender-application-control/windows-defender-application-control`.

Exploit protection

To reduce the likelihood of attacks on operating system processes, as well as individual applications, we can enable exploit protection in our environments.

Like most of these settings, you can configure this one through multiple avenues. In the following screenshots, you'll see what it looks like when these avenues are accessed individually via your Windows 10 machine's start menu | **Windows Security** | **App & browser control**. Here, I will select **Exploit protection** settings to see what's configurable there:

Isolated browsing

Windows Defender Application Guard opens Microsoft Edge in an isolated browsing environment to better protect your device and data from malware.

Install Windows Defender Application Guard

Learn more

Exploit protection

Exploit protection is built into Windows 10 to help protect your device against attacks. Out of the box, your device is already set up with the protection settings that work best for most people.

Exploit protection settings

Privacy Statement

Learn more

As you can see, we're able to configure system settings (operating system) and program settings (individual applications):

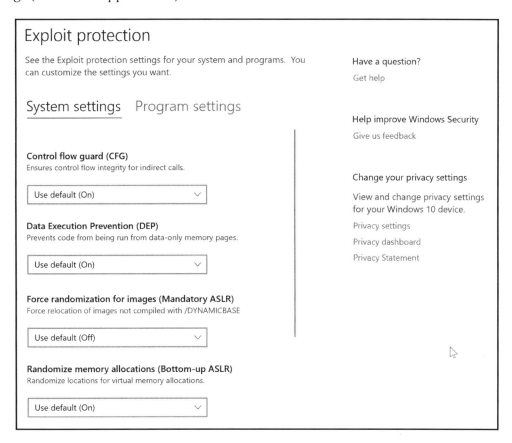

Network protection

Network protection allows you to block users who are attempting to access malicious or blocked URLs from utilizing apps.

In this section, I'll demonstrate configuring a device profile for Windows 10 machines that illustrates the broad spectrum of Microsoft Defender settings that are available during configuration. Let's get started:

1. First, we need to create a new profile for Windows 10 machines and set the profile type to **Endpoint protection** (machine). Our settings will provide many Microsoft Defender options.

2. Next, select **Windows Defender Exploit Guard**:

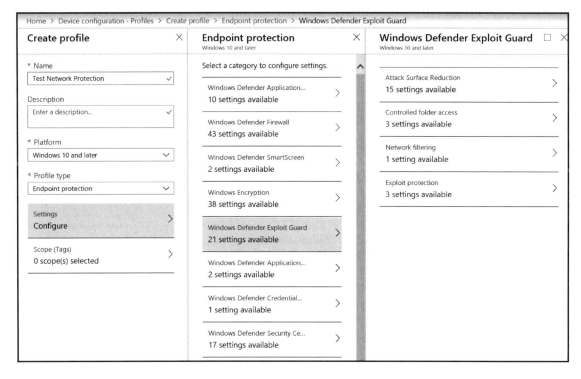

3. Now, under **Network filtering**, we can enable network protection. The **Audit** option only logs potential risks, whereas **Enable** will actively block and log, thereby sending notifications to the Action Center:

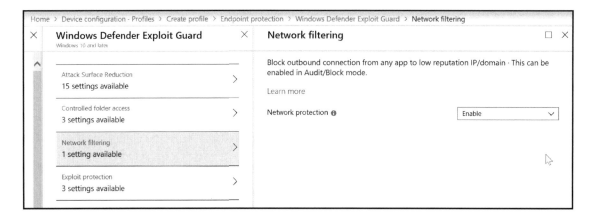

Controlled folder access

Controlled folder access can restrict suspicious or malicious apps from making changes to the folders you want to protect.

If you were to enable this via Group Policy, you'd go to **Group Policy Management Editor | Computer configuration | Administrative templates | Windows components | Windows defender Antivirus | Windows Defender Exploit Guard | Controlled folder access**. Open **Configure Controlled folder access** and enable this feature by setting **Block** from the option drop-down menu.

That's a lot of steps. Alternatively, you could run the following PowerShell command:

```
Set-MpPreference -EnableControlledFolderAccess Enabled
```

Network firewall

The last feature we'll cover when we wish to reduce our attack surface is the Windows Defender Firewall. This firewall provides two-way traffic filtering on your network. From here, you can do the following:

- Restrict network access to certain store apps.
- Block client computers from sending traffic to backend servers.
- Restrict any unsolicited communication from backend servers to frontend servers.

Your options are vast and will vary, depending on your needs.

 You can find the various configuration options and more information about each of these actions at `https://docs.microsoft.com/en-us/windows/security/threat-protection/microsoft-defender-atp/configure-attack-surface-reduction`.

Now, let's explore what next-generation protection is and how it helps us to manage the security of our environment.

Next-generation protection

Next-generation protection refers to utilizing Windows Defender Antivirus, specifically for near-instant blocking of new threats. As security threats are identified, your environment is protected.

Cloud-provided protection shortens the delivery time of security monitoring and threat mitigation in your environment. It is enabled by default.

Real-time, always on, behavioral-based, and **heuristic protection** can be configured to provide you with big data-backed, research-informed protection. You can disallow toolbars, add-ins, fake antivirus apps, and more as they emerge globally.

You can also choose who your end users will interact with. Should they see notifications? Should they be able to override the settings you deploy?

 You can read more about next-generation protection at https://docs. microsoft.com/en-au/windows/security/threat-protection/windows-defender-antivirus/configure-windows-defender-antivirus-features.

Summary

In this chapter, we covered how to plan out a Windows Defender ATP solution, how to configure our preferences, how to implement Windows Defender ATP policies, and how to enable and configure the security features of Windows 10 Enterprise.

We learned that Windows Defender ATP and Microsoft Defender ATP are the same thing and that, in time, the exam may be updated as well. Remember that they're currently used interchangeably.

When planning our Windows Defender ATP solution, we learned that our devices must be running Windows 7 or later, and that any servers must be running 2008 R2 or later.

When configuring preferences, we considered the possibilities that the Secure Score dashboard provides, learned about Microsoft Threat Experts capabilities, and integrated Cloud App Security, which we learn about in Chapter 5, *Implementing Cloud App Security (CAS)*.

We also learned that we can enable conditional access by utilizing Microsoft Defender with Intune.

Finally, we explored how we can reduce the attack surface of our environment and learned about next-generation protection and how it makes sure we're protected in real time as threats are identified by Microsoft security experts.

In the next chapter, we'll discover the security reports and alerts that are available to you as an administrator.

Questions

1. You need to configure conditional access for devices that are marked as compliant according to Windows Defender ATP threat levels. Which statements need to be true for this to work? (Mark all that apply.)

   A. Devices are Azure-AD joined.
   B. Devices are enrolled in Intune MDM.
   C. The Intune compliance policy is configured.
   D. The Azure AD Conditional Access policy is configured.

2. In the Windows Defender ATP portal, you're viewing the machine list and need to determine which security groups `Computer1` is a member of. When you select it, you see the following information:

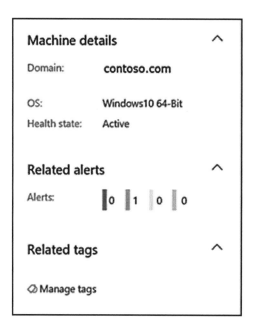

Groups are defined by the following characteristics:

Rank	Machine Group	Members
1	Group 1	Tag equals admin
2	Group 2	Domain equals `contoso.com` and the OS is Windows 10
3	Group 3	Domain equals `contoso.com`
Last	Ungrouped machines (default)	All others

`Computer1` belongs to which group(s)? (Select all that apply.)

A. Group 1
B. Group 2
C. Group 3
D. Ungrouped

Further reading

- **Planning our Windows Defender ATP solution**:
    - *Microsoft Defender Advanced Threat Protection*: `https://docs.microsoft.com/en-us/windows/security/threat-protection/microsoft-defender-atp/microsoft-defender-advanced-threat-protection`

- **Configuring our preferences**:
    - *Configuring and managing Microsoft Defender ATP capabilities*: `https://docs.microsoft.com/en-us/windows/security/threat-protection/microsoft-defender-atp/onboard`
    - *Configuring Conditional Access in Microsoft Defender ATP*: `https://docs.microsoft.com/en-us/windows/security/threat-protection/microsoft-defender-atp/configure-conditional-access`
    - *Configuring Microsoft Cloud App Security in Microsoft Defender ATP*: `https://docs.microsoft.com/en-us/windows/security/threat-protection/microsoft-defender-atp/microsoft-cloud-app-security-config`

- **Implementing Windows Defender ATP policies**:
  - *Enforcing compliance for Microsoft Defender ATP with Conditional Access in Intune*: https://docs.microsoft.com/en-us/intune/advanced-threat-protection

- **Enabling and configuring the security features of Windows 10 Enterprise**:
  - *Configuring attack surface reduction*: https://docs.microsoft.com/en-us/windows/security/threat-protection/microsoft-defender-atp/configure-attack-surface-reduction
  - *Inside out: Getting to know the advanced technologies at the core of Microsoft Defender ATP next-generation protection*: https://www.microsoft.com/security/blog/2019/06/24/inside-out-get-to-know-the-advanced-technologies-at-the-core-of-microsoft-defender-atp-next-generation-protection/
  - *Configuring Windows Defender Antivirus features*: https://docs.microsoft.com/en-us/windows/security/threat-protection/windows-defender-antivirus/configure-windows-defender-antivirus-features

Managing Security Reports and Alerts

8

In this chapter, we'll be taking a look at the management of various security reports and alerts. The Service Assurance Dashboard lets you address the concerns of executive stakeholders by being able to provide quickly third-party audits of Office 365 services and documents on Microsoft's security practices. You can also configure your Microsoft 365 security and Azure AD Identity Protection alerts to keep you informed of important changes in your environment.

The following exam topics will each be covered in this chapter:

- Managing the Service Assurance Dashboard
- Microsoft Secure Score and Azure AD Identity Secure Score
- Tracing and reporting on Azure AD Identity Protection
- Microsoft 365 security alerts
- Azure AD Identity Protection dashboard and alerts

Let's begin with a look at the Service Assurance Dashboard.

Managing the Service Assurance Dashboard

O365 Enterprise E3 and E5 subscribers can access the Service Assurance Dashboard, which gives insight into the security practices Microsoft employs to protect your data stored in O365. You'll also find audits performed by third-party entities. This kind of information can be helpful in navigating compliance and risk discussions when there are concerns about storing and managing data in the cloud.

In this section, we'll cover the following topics:

- Access the Service Assurance Dashboard
- Compliance Manager
- Granting access to others

Let's start with how you access the Service Assurance Dashboard.

Accessing the Service Assurance Dashboard

You'll find the Service Assurance Dashboard in the Microsoft 365 Security & Compliance Center. This dashboard provides documentation and information about industry compliance and regulations, such as how your data is stored. Let's perform the following steps:

1. Go to `protection.office.com`.
2. Select **Service assurance** from the left navigation pane. If accessing for the first time, you'll need to set your region and industry first to make sure you're accessing the most appropriate resources:

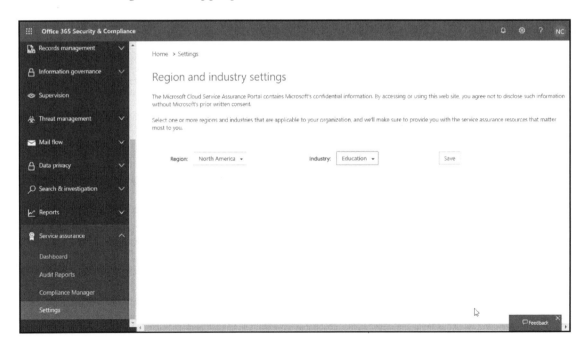

3. Once you've saved those settings, and as seen in the previous screenshot, you can now choose to view **Dashboard** or **Audit Reports** (third-party audit and trust reports detailing how your data is stored and protected) from the left under **Service assurance**. The following screenshot shows the dashboard which provides information about available tools.

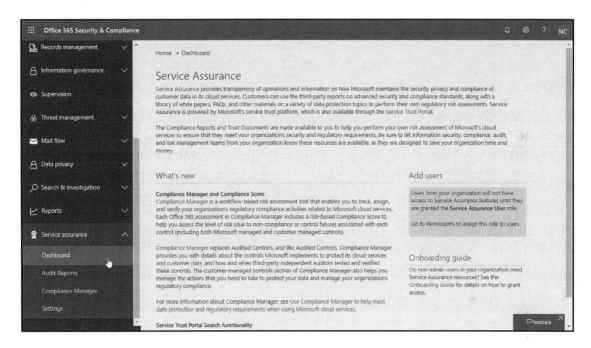

The final option under **Service assurance** before **Settings** is **Compliance Manager**, which we'll cover next.

Compliance Manager

Compliance Manager is another dashboard you can access through the **Security & Compliance Center | Service assurance**. You could also just navigate directly to `servicetrust.microsoft.com/ComplianceManager`. Once you're there, you'll see a dashboard similar to the following:

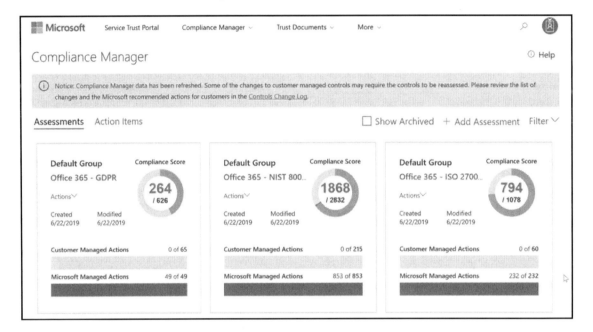

From here, you're able to view the compliance topics Microsoft manages, and set up your own customer-managed assessments as well. Click on any of the hyperlinked assessments, and expand any of its sections to assign specific actions to individuals. The following screenshot shows an expanded section regarding **Access Control**:

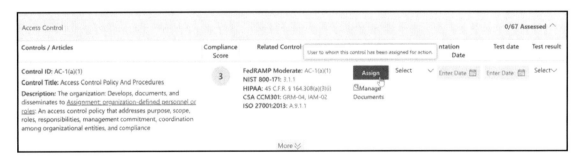

Once you click **Assign**, you can choose to whom to assign action items, and email those individuals directly from the action item dialog seen in the following screenshot:

Anything assigned to users appears under their individual **Action Items** link, assuming they have access to the dashboard.

As a global administrator, you can see most dashboards and reports. However, it is likely that you'll be asked to allow someone who is *not* a global administrator to view a dashboard. In the next subsection, we'll cover how to grant someone access to view just the Service Assurance Dashboard.

Granting access to others

To allow others to access **Service assurance** and perform assurance reviews, you'll need to add them to the Service assurance user group in the Security & Compliance Center (protection.office.com | **Permissions**). These permission roles are likely to appear in the exam. Take some time to explore them and what they permit.

Following is a screenshot illustrating the process of modifying members of the **Service Assurance User** role group. Note how, once selected, we're given a description of what the permission role allows. Then we click **Edit** in the **Members** section to modify group members:

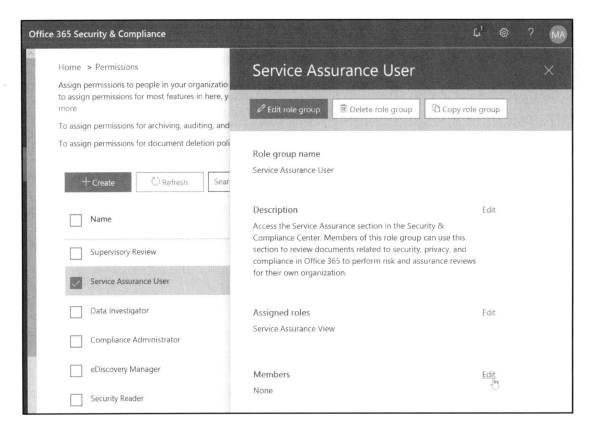

Next, let's take a quick look at secure scores.

Microsoft Secure Score and Azure AD Identity Secure Score

The Microsoft Secure Score breaks down the various settings and features you've applied (or haven't) throughout your tenants or security tasks you've completed. A point value is given to these settings and tasks, and the total of points earned becomes your total secure score. Your secure score comes with a list of specific improvement actions you can take to improve your score. Your score is divided into **Identity**, **Data**, **Device**, **Apps**, and **Infrastructure** categories as seen in the overview that follows:

You can access the Microsoft Secure Score at `security.microsoft.com/securescore`.

The Azure AD Identity Secure Score, one factor in the overall Microsoft Secure Score, gives you an idea of actions you could take to improve your overall security practices when it comes specifically to identity management. For example, as seen in the following screenshot, we could require **Multi-Factor Authentication (MFA)** for Azure AD privileged roles and gain 50 points as a result. Each improvement action can be expanded to tell you your current score details and to provide guidance on making the suggested improvement:

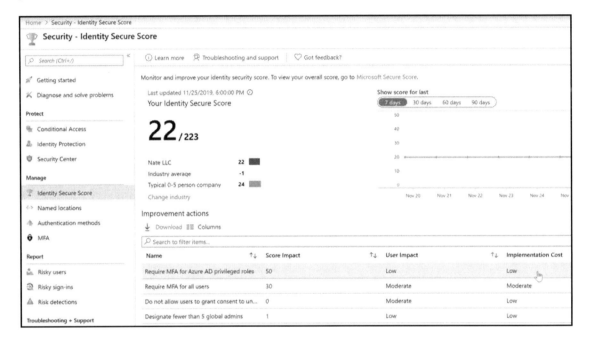

You can access the Azure AD Identity Secure Score from portal.azure.com | **Azure Active Directory** | **Security** | **Identity Secure Score** (on the left navigation menu under **Manage**).

In the next section, we'll learn about tracing and reporting on Azure AD Identity Protection.

Tracing and reporting on Azure AD Identity Protection

Azure AD Identity Protection empowers administrators to automate responses to suspicious user identity-related activities. We'll look at the following topics related to Azure AD Identity Protection:

- Investigate risk events and vulnerabilities
- Settings and alerts

Investigating risk events and vulnerabilities

In the Azure AD Identity Protection dashboard (`portal.azure.com` | search for `Azure AD Identity Protection`), you'll notice some reports on the left, including **Risky users** in which Azure has flagged suspicious activity for your review. At a glance, you can see which have been remediated (or not) and what the level of risk is:

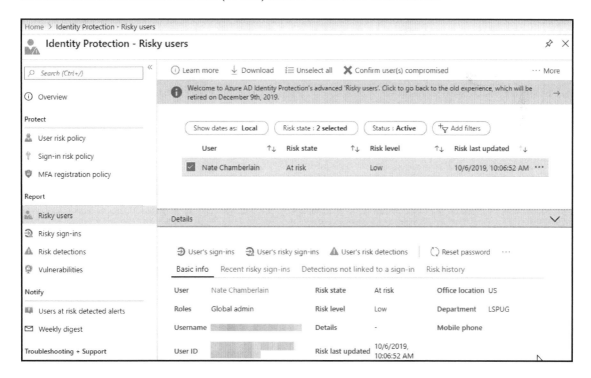

Risky sign-ins would list any sign-in activity deemed risky and give you all of the identifying information for the machine, sign-in location, risk type, and so on.

Risk detections will show you when users are signing in from anonymous IP addresses, leaked credentials, sign-ins from infected devices, and so on:

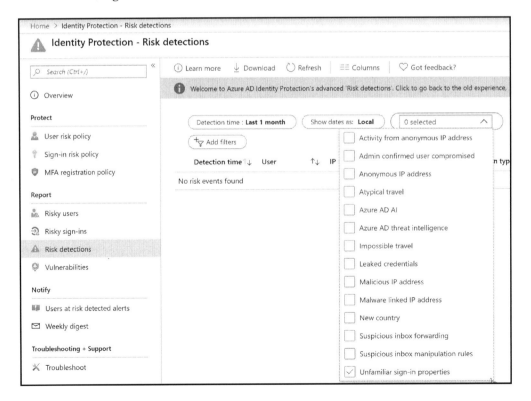

Read more about **Risk events** at `https://docs.microsoft.com/en-us/` `azure/active-directory/reports-monitoring/concept-risk-events`.

Vulnerabilities displays issues you could address to improve your security, such as enabling **MFA** for users, reducing the number of global or redundant administrators, identifying and remediating unmanaged cloud apps, and so on:

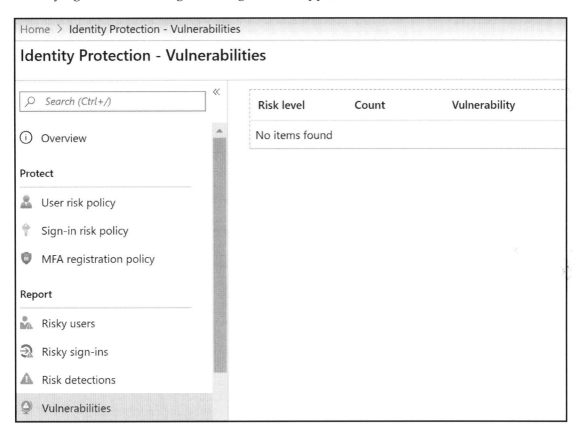

Now let's see what we can configure for settings and alerts.

Settings and alerts

Under **Notify**, you'll find two notification options:

- Users at risk detected alerts
- Weekly digest

This requires the Azure AD Premium P2 license, which is available as a standalone subscription or included in Microsoft 365 E5, EMS E5, or Microsoft 365 Security E5 subscriptions. **Users at risk detected alerts** allow you to select individuals to receive email alerts when low, medium, or high risk events occur. The following shows the configuration screen for the **Users at risk detected alerts** notification:

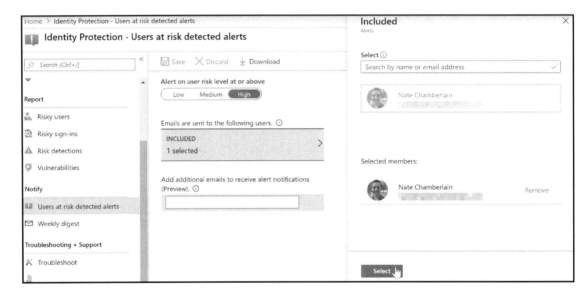

Weekly digest combines the investigative categories of users flagged for risk, risk events, and vulnerabilities and sends those to selected parties on a weekly basis in a summary. The summary figures in the email message will link to the relevant dashboards in Azure AD Identity Protection. The following screenshot shows the configuration screen for setting up the weekly digest, a manager request scenario you may encounter on the exam:

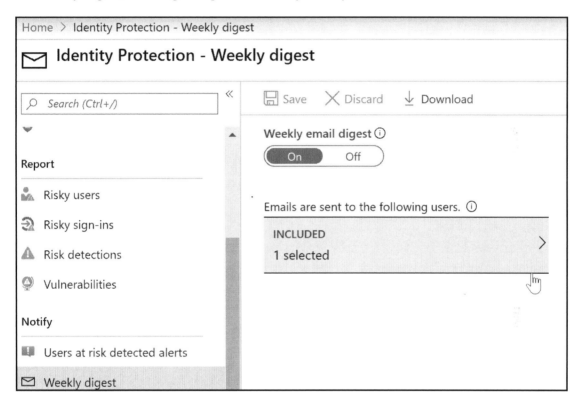

In the next section, let's look at Microsoft 365 security alerts.

Microsoft 365 security alerts

In the Security & Compliance Center (`protection.office.com`), you can select **Alerts** |
View alerts from the left navigation pane to view, filter, and resolve alerts:

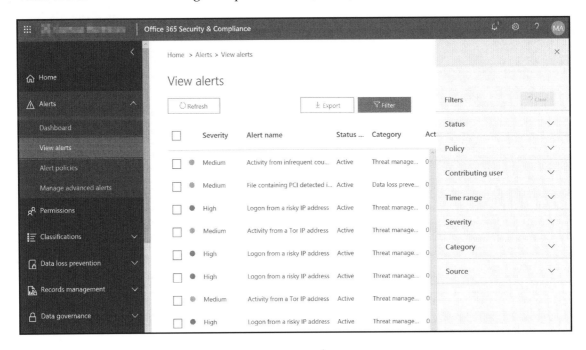

To view more detail on an alert, check the box to its left. This opens a pane with more detail and the option to resolve it as seen in the screenshot that follows:

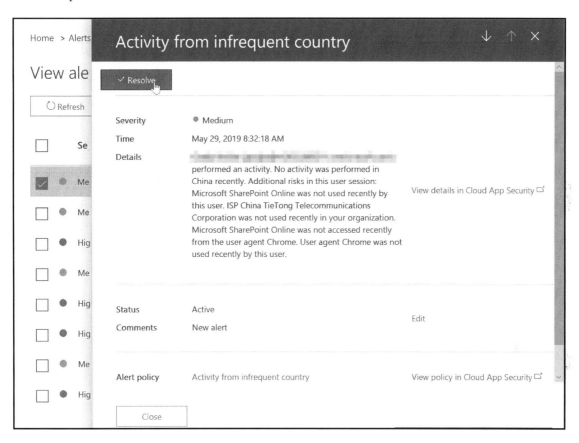

If you select **Resolve** on an alert, you're able to modify its status and add additional comments. For the status drop-down list, you can choose from the following to help track the status of the alert:

- Keep it **Active** and just add comments: No change, except perhaps notes.
- **Investigating**: Currently being looked into.
- **Resolved**: Action has been taken so that the alert is no longer a concern.
- **Dismissed**: The alert is a false positive or no action will be taken.

As seen in the following screenshot you can choose the alert status from a dropdown, enter accompanying comments, and save to update the alert accordingly.

Under **Alert policies**, you can adjust existing policies (and some default policies). For each policy, you'll configure the severity, category, conditions, actions, and so on. In the following example, the policy is default and is looking for anomalous activity in external file sharing:

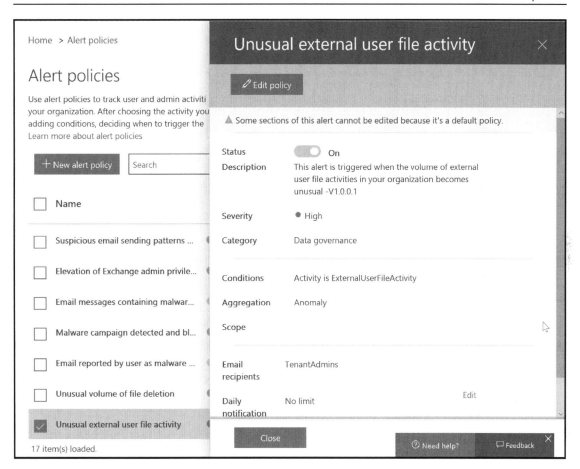

Here's a list of other activities (conditions) you could base a policy on. For the exam, be sure to become familiar with the types of policies you can create with these actions:

Common user activities	File and folder activities	File sharing activities	Synchronization events	Site administration activities
Detected malware in an email message	Accessed file	Accepted access request	Allowed computer to sync files	Added exempt user agent
Phishing email detected at time of delivery	Checked in file	Accepted sharing invitation	Blocked computer from syncing files	Added site collection admin

User submitted email	Checked out file	Created a company shareable link	Downloaded files to computer	Added user or group to SharePoint group
Detected malware in file	Copied file	Created access request	Downloaded file changes to computer	Allowed user to create groups
Shared file or folder	Deleted file	Created an anonymous link	Uploaded files to document library	Changed exempt user agents
Created mail forward/redirect rule	Discarded file checkout	Created sharing invitation	Uploaded file changes to document library	Changed a sharing policy
Any file or folder activity	Downloaded file	Denied access request		Created group
Changed file or folder	Modified file	Removed a company shareable link		Created Sent To connection
Shared file externally	Moved file	Removed an anonymous link		Created site collection
Granted Exchange admin permission	Renamed file	Shared file, folder, or site		Deleted group
Granted mailbox permission	Restored file	Updated an anonymous link		Deleted Sent To connection
External user file activity	Uploaded file	Used an anonymous link		Enabled document preview
DLP policy match				Enabled legacy workflow
An eDiscovery search was started or exported				Enabled Office on Demand
				Enabled RSS feeds
				Enabled result source for people searches

				Modified site permissions
				Removed user or group from SharePoint group
				Renamed site
				Requested site admin permissions
				Set host site
				Updated group

A good example of an alert you might be asked to create would be one that notifies someone when a file from a particularly sensitive site, or with a certain name, is shared externally. The following screenshot shows the configuration of an alert's trigger and scope:

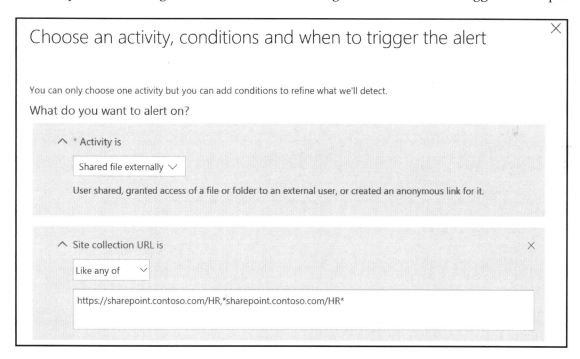

Manage advanced alerts takes you to the Cloud App Security dashboard we discussed in a previous chapter.

In the next section, we'll look into the Azure AD Identity Protection dashboard and its alerts.

Azure AD Identity Protection dashboard and alerts

The Azure AD Identity Protection dashboard allows you to identify and respond to risk events automatically using policies, or manually. In the following subsections, we'll explore both of these possibilities:

- Automatically close or resolve risk events
- Manually close risk events

We'll start with how you can use policies to automatically close or resolve risk events.

Automatically closing or resolving risk events

Under PROTECT on the left navigation of Azure AD Identity Protection, you'll notice three policy-like configurations: **User risk policy**, **Sign-in risk policy**, and **MFA registration policy**:

For each you will configure:

- Which users/groups to include or exclude
- Conditions: Sensitivity/risk level (low and above, medium and above, or high)
- Controls/Access or what should happen if the risk level is met for the selected users
- Review (illustrates estimated impact of the policy)

The following shows a user risk policy and each of the aforementioned configurations:

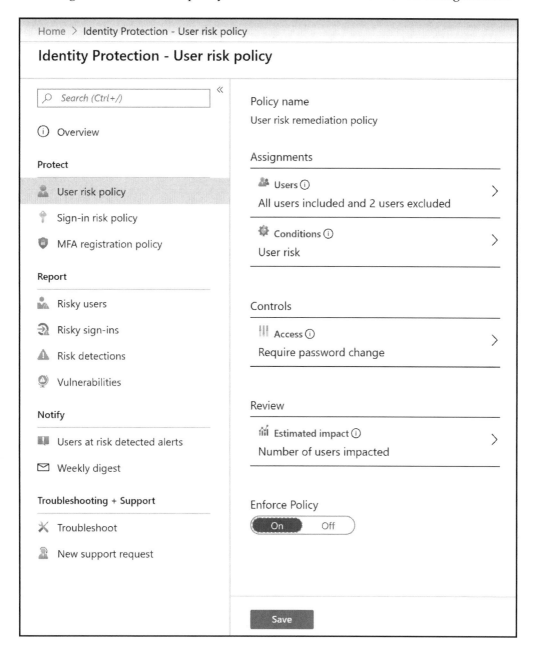

Under **User risk policy** you can set up a conditional statement that, based on the risk level, automatically remediates user risk issues:

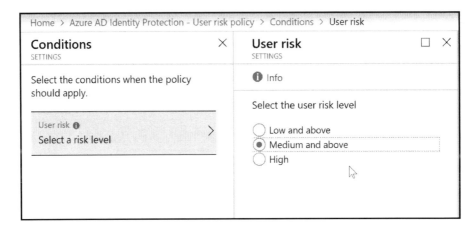

If that condition is met, you can do the following:

- Block access or allow access
- Require password change

Sign-in risk policy works nearly the same, but, instead of requiring a password change, you can require MFA. So, for example, if a user is signing in from an unknown IP address, you could have them authenticate their login with the extra steps involved in MFA. In the following screenshot, you can see the **Access** configuration setting for an Azure AD Identity Protection sign-in risk policy:

The final option is **MFA registration policy**. This one is the simplest, as you just pick the users/groups who should have MFA enabled and who, if any, should be excluded. Risk level, or any condition, is not a factor.

Now let's look at the option of manually closing risk events.

Manually closing risk events

To manually resolve risk events, select a risk event or flagged user, then a specific flagged sign-in. Once the pane opens with details of the event, you have the following options for actions to take:

- **Resolve**: You took action outside of Identity Protection to resolve/close the risk.
- **Mark as false positive**: Closes the event and improves machine learning by reporting an incorrect risk event.
- **Ignore**: You have not taken action, but don't want the event on your list.
- **Reactivate**: Make a resolved, false positive, or ignored risk event active again.

The following screenshot shows details of a risk event that has been closed, showing its resolution was a changed password:

Summary

In this chapter, we covered reporting and alerts; these are topics you'll find on the exam, including the following:

- Managing the Service Assurance Dashboard
- Tracing and reporting on Azure AD Identity Protection
- Microsoft 365 security alerts
- Azure AD Identity Protection dashboard and alerts

We learned that the Service Assurance Dashboard can be shared with others who are not global admins, and that the two dashboards when combined with Compliance Manager give us insight into knowing how our data is stored and how the various services we use are made compliant with industry regulations. The Compliance Manager dashboard also allows us the ability to assign responsibility for generic or custom compliance topics to users in our organization.

The Azure AD Identity Protection allows us to investigate risk events, such as anomalous sign-in events and alerts, and to configure our notification settings for them.

We found which alerts and dashboards are available in the Microsoft 365 Security & Compliance Center, and how to configure alerts and associated policies.

We learned that we can either automatically resolve risk events in Azure AD Identity Protection by creating policies, or we can manually resolve them. In reality, we would be using a combination of automatic and manual resolution.

This Chapter concludes `Section 2`, *Microsoft 365 Security and Threat Management*. We'll begin `Section 3`, *Microsoft 365 Governance and Compliance,* in the next chapter by configuring **data loss prevention** (**DLP**).

Questions

1. One of your organization's security administrators is reviewing a report from Azure AD that shows recent sign-ins and their locations. The report will be used to determine proper configuration for blocking access from untrusted networks and requiring MFA for high-risk sign-ins. What should you recommend as part of the solution?

    A. Azure AD Identity Protection Sign-in risk policy
    B. Azure AD Identity Protection User risk policy
    C. Azure AD Identity Protection weekly digest email
    D. Azure AD | Monitoring | Audit logs

2. Your HR director wants to be notified whenever somebody adds a SharePoint site collection administrator to their talent acquisition site collection. What should you configure for them?

    A. Azure AD Identity Protection alert
    B. Security & Compliance alert
    C. SharePoint admin center settings
    D. Security & Compliance audit logs

Further reading

- **Managing the Service Assurance Dashboard**:
    - *Service assurance in the Security & Compliance Center*: https://docs.microsoft.com/en-us/office365/securitycompliance/service-assurance

- **Microsoft Secure Score and Azure AD Identity Secure Score**:
    - *Microsoft Secure Score*: https://docs.microsoft.com/en-us/microsoft-365/security/mtp/microsoft-secure-score
    - *What is the identity secure score in Azure Active Directory?*: https://docs.microsoft.com/en-us/azure/active-directory/fundamentals/identity-secure-score

- **Tracing and reporting on Azure AD Identity Protection**:
    - *Risky sign-ins report in the Azure Active Directory portal*: `https://docs.microsoft.com/en-us/azure/active-directory/reports-monitoring/concept-risky-sign-ins`
    - *What is Azure Active Directory Identity Protection?*: `https://docs.microsoft.com/en-us/azure/active-directory/identity-protection/overview`

- **Microsoft 365 security alerts**:
    - *Alerts in the Office 365 Security & Compliance Center*: `https://docs.microsoft.com/en-us/office365/securitycompliance/alerts`

- **Azure AD Identity Protection dashboard and alerts**:
    - *Azure Active Directory Identity Protection - security overview*: `https://docs.microsoft.com/en-us/azure/active-directory/identity-protection/security-overview`
    - *How To: Close active risk events*: `https://docs.microsoft.com/en-us/azure/active-directory/identity-protection/howto-close-active-risk-events`

3
Section 3: Microsoft 365 Governance Compliance

This section will cover **data loss prevention** (**DLP**), data governance, and the auditing tools that you can use to secure your data. These topics make up 35-40% of the MS-101 exam.

This section includes the following chapters:

- Chapter 9, *Configuring Data Loss Prevention (DLP)*
- Chapter 10, *Implementing Azure Information Protection (AIP)*
- Chapter 11, *Managing Data Governance*
- Chapter 12, *Managing Auditing*
- Chapter 13, *Managing eDiscovery*

9
Configuring Data Loss Prevention (DLP)

Data loss prevention (**DLP**) tools in Microsoft 365 work cross-tenant so that you can protect your data as it moves from service to service. In this chapter, you'll learn how to configure policies and settings so that they match your organization's security and compliance requirements. For example, you may have a scenario in which you need to prevent any **payment card industry** (**PCI**) data from leaving the organization. DLP policies can help you meet that requirement.

In this chapter, we will cover the following exam topics:

- Configuring DLP policies
- Designing data retention policies in Microsoft 365
- Monitoring and managing DLP policy matches
- Managing DLP exceptions

Let's begin by configuring DLP policies.

Configuring DLP policies

DLP policies are likely to appear on the MS-101 exam. In this section, we'll look at reviewing existing policies and creating new ones from the **Microsoft 365 Security & Compliance Center**. Let's get started:

1. From the **Security & Compliance Center**, select **Data loss prevention** | **Policy** to view your currently active policies and start creating new ones:

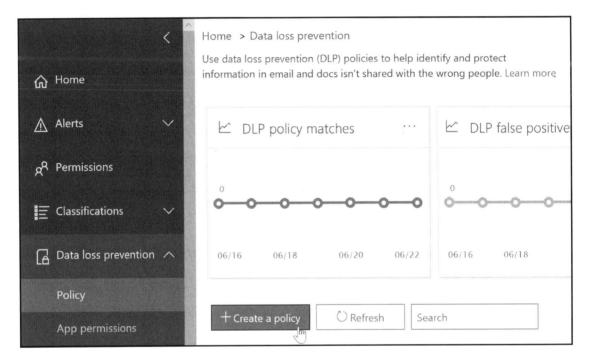

When creating policies, you'll notice that you can start from a DLP policy template (such as HIPAA for protected health data, or PII for personally identifiable information) or create a policy from scratch using **Custom**. Even if you use a template, you're able to modify it later. Templates simply get you started with pre-selected data identifiers:

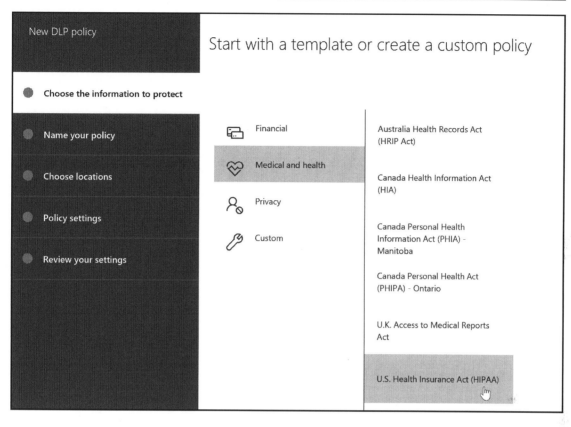

New DLP policy

Start with a template or create a custom policy

● Choose the information to protect

○ Name your policy

○ Choose locations

○ Policy settings

○ Review your settings

Financial

Medical and health

Privacy

Custom

Australia Health Records Act (HRIP Act)

Canada Health Information Act (HIA)

Canada Personal Health Information Act (PHIA) - Manitoba

Canada Personal Health Act (PHIPA) - Ontario

U.K. Access to Medical Reports Act

U.S. Health Insurance Act (HIPAA)

2. Once you've decided to use a DLP policy template or create a custom policy, click **Next** in the **New DLP policy** wizard to name and describe your policy. Once you're done, click **Next**.

3. In the **Choose locations** section, you'll be prompted to protect data across Exchange, Teams, OneDrive, and SharePoint, though you can choose specific locations. Maybe you only want to create an Exchange-specific policy, for example, where you'll respond to DLP incidents differently than you may do in SharePoint.

You may also want to get granular and create a special DLP policy for a specific SharePoint site. **Let me choose specific locations** will allow you that granularity, shown selected here:

After selecting **Let me choose specific locations**, you can then choose specific apps and choose which components you wish to include and/or exclude, as shown in the following screenshot:

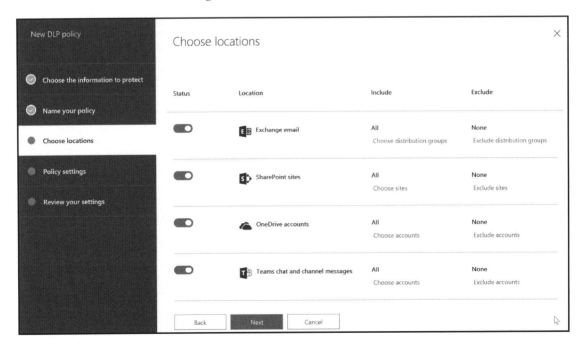

Retention labels aren't currently supported for Exchange as a location. You'd need to remove Exchange as a location, or not use retention labels for Exchange DLP policies at all.

4. The next step allows you to customize the template's data types or begin choosing data types if you chose **Custom**. In the following screenshot, you can select **Edit** to adjust or add to the data types automatically suggested for HIPAA:

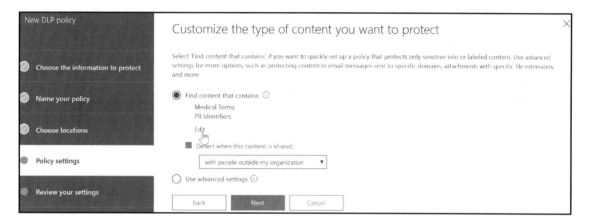

When you choose **Edit**, you can see what's included in the template you chose (if any) and/or begin adding conditions and groups of data types to look for as seen here:

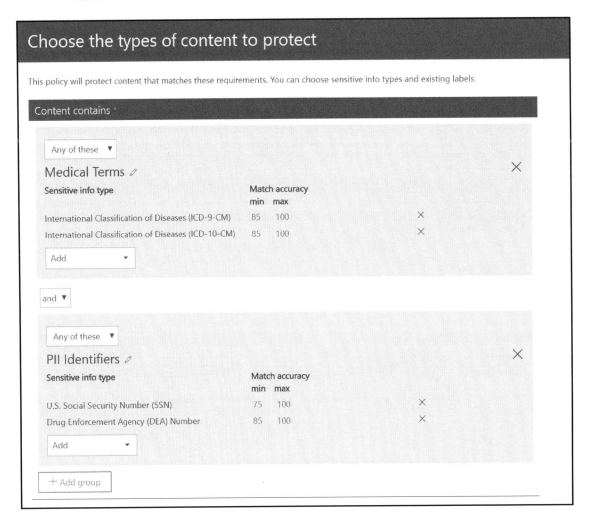

If you choose **Use advanced settings** on the **Policy settings** screen, you're able to create rules including conditions, exceptions, actions, user notifications, user override abilities, incident reports, and more.

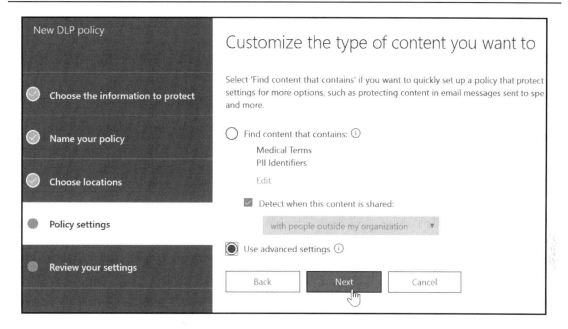

However you configure your rules (by template or from scratch), click **Save** and/or click **Next** to continue through the New DLP policy wizard.

5. Once you've finished creating or modifying rules, you'll find a screen asking which action to take when sensitive information is detected:

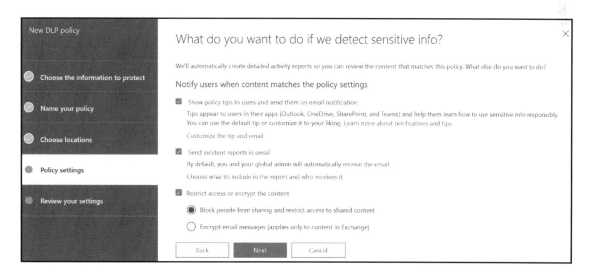

You can choose to show policy tips to users who are involved, letting them know in-context when there's a potential DLP policy conflict. You could also send an email. Both policy tips and emails are customizable on this screen. Notice the ability also to send incident reports, or restrict access and encrypt content

6. Next you can allow everyone to see sensitive content, or restrict it to only those within your organization. And for policy tips, users can either be allowed to override with or without justification as seen in the following screenshot:

7. On this final **Policy settings** screen, you'll choose whether you're ready to put the policy into effect immediately, you wish to test it first (with or without active policy tips), or keep it off until a later date. Click **Next**:

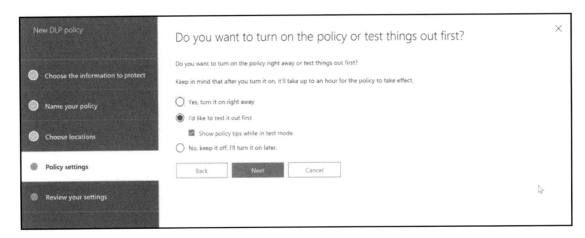

8. The final screen, **Review your settings**, provides you with a user-friendly glimpse at what you've created. You can confirm that the settings you've configured are correct in the **Policy Settings** section. If something looks like it's incorrect, just click **Edit** to go back to that part of the configuration wizard and correct it. Click **Create** when you're finished:

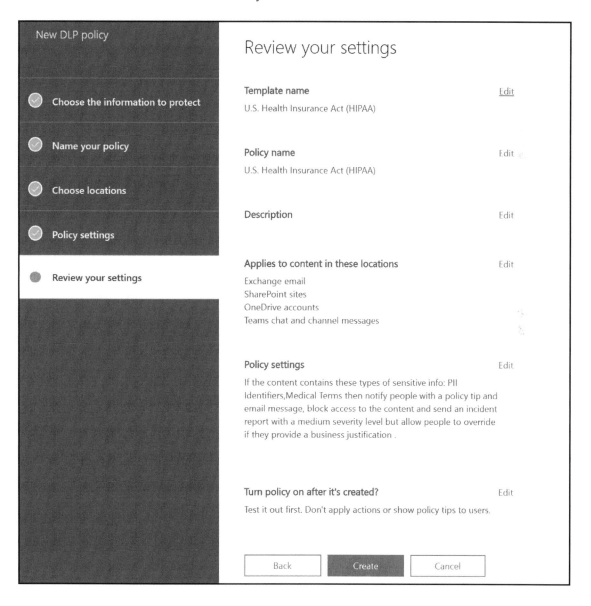

New DLP policy

Choose the information to protect

Name your policy

Choose locations

Policy settings

Review your settings

Review your settings

Template name   Edit
U.S. Health Insurance Act (HIPAA)

Policy name   Edit
U.S. Health Insurance Act (HIPAA)

Description   Edit

Applies to content in these locations   Edit
Exchange email
SharePoint sites
OneDrive accounts
Teams chat and channel messages

Policy settings   Edit
If the content contains these types of sensitive info: PII
Identifiers,Medical Terms then notify people with a policy tip and
email message, block access to the content and send an incident
report with a medium severity level but allow people to override
if they provide a business justification .

Turn policy on after it's created?   Edit
Test it out first. Don't apply actions or show policy tips to users.

Back   Create   Cancel

Back on the **Policies** screen, you'll see all of your policies and any matches on the graphic summary cards. You can select any policy to review it at a high level or edit it:

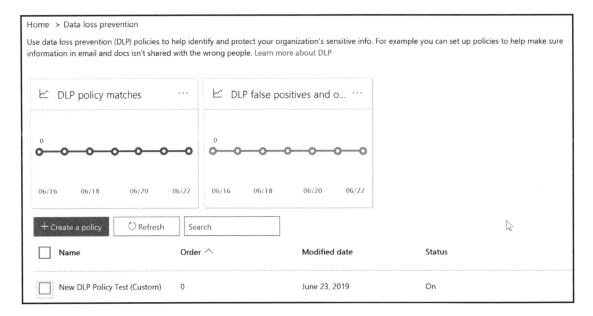

Once you have more than one DLP policy, you can configure their **Order/Rank**. In the event of multiple applicable policies, the *most restrictive* actions will apply. If there are multiple policies with the same level of restriction, it will go with the *highest priority* among them.

In the next section, we will design data retention policies.

Designing data retention policies in Microsoft 365

Retention policies help ensure that your organization is mitigating risks that are concerned with breach or litigation by retaining data for the appropriate period of time based on its type. They also help you comply with industry and internal policies regarding data retention. Furthermore, because all of the content should have a defined lifespan, retention policies also help keep your data current by keeping it for as long as it's needed and then deleting the data at the end of its retention period.

You can create retention policies in either the Microsoft 365 Compliance Center (`compliance.microsoft.com` | **Policies** | **Retention**) or the Office 365 Security & Compliance Center (`protection.office.com` | **Data governance** | **Retention**).

With retention policies, you'll be dealing with two important topics:

- **Labels** (auto-assigned via a policy or manually assigned by users)
- **Label policies** (to publish labels, collect justification for their removal, and so on):

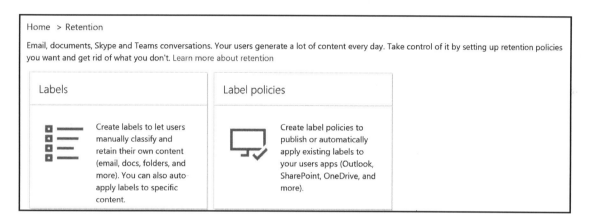

Labels and label policies can be either of the following:

- Sensitivity labels/label policies (deals with protecting data based on its content)
- Retention labels/label policies (deals with data life cycles and keeping documents for a defined period of time)

Let's start by looking at labels.

Labels

Labels allow you to classify your content in meaningful ways and associate it with an action.

When creating a new sensitivity label, you can configure the following:

- Content marking (the headers, footers, or watermarks that are applied to documents)

- Encryption (modify permissions and the duration you can access them for, as well as offline access)
- Endpoint data loss prevention (utilize Windows Information Protection to prevent data leaks on Windows devices)
- Auto-labelling (automatically apply or suggest that the user applies a specific label to a document based on its contents. If suggesting a label, you can customize the policy tip that appears to the user. Requires the **Azure Information Protection** (**AIP**) unified labeling client to be installed.)

 Endpoint data loss prevention requires additional prerequisites. Please take a look at them at `https://docs.microsoft.com/en-us/Office365/SecurityCompliance/sensitivity-labels#important-prerequisites`.

When you create a new retention label, different options will be available to you, including retention/deletion details and file plan descriptors that help inform users why a label is being applied to their content:

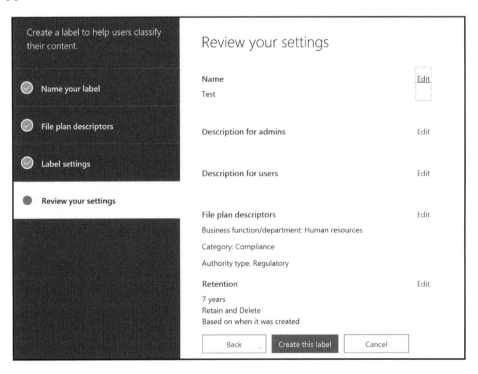

Now, let's look at label policies.

Label policies

Policies allow you to publish the labels you've set up for specific users or groups so that they can be used within specific contexts, such as O365 or Exchange (or both).

You can set label policies so that a certain label is always applied for a specific user or group by default. Perhaps your CEO needs *highly confidential* applied to every email. If no default is chosen, the label is simply available for the user to apply manually.

An additional feature within policy configuration is the ability to require justification for removing an applied label.

Sensitivity label policies are applied to users and groups (making them available for usage).

Retention label policies, on the other hand, are applied to locations (SharePoint, Exchange, and so on) and have additional settings in terms of retention/deletion period details, such as keeping the policy for a period of time and then deleting it. You could also have your policies set up so that users can delete files whenever they wish. However, the policy would definitely delete anything older than a defined age based on its creation or last modified date:

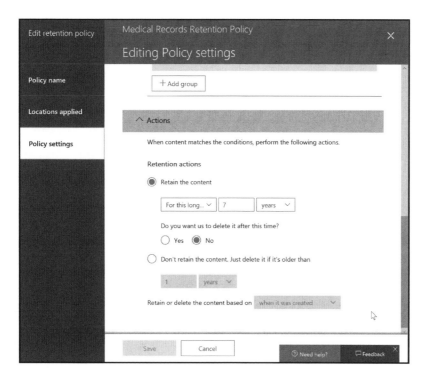

The following are some notes regarding retention policies:

- SharePoint files that have been modified after a retention label has been applied to them are copied and moved to the **Preservation Hold Library** (this isn't created until it's needed). The most recent/edited version will still live where it was found. Only site collection administrators can see this library.
- Email and public folders that have been modified after a label has been applied can be found in the `Recoverable Items` folder, viewable by admins.
- When an item is deleted in SharePoint, or when its retention policy expires, it is still recoverable for 93 days from the first- or second-stage recycle bin.
- Skype messages are stored in Exchange as a *conversation* data type. Your policies can apply to emails or conversations in Exchange.
- Retention policies for O365 groups include the site and associated mailbox.
- DLP policies are more robust than retention policies, meaning that, if an item is identified as sensitive through a DLP policy but you remove the sensitive content, the label can be retracted automatically. However, with retention policies, even if sensitive content is removed, it doesn't reassess and automatically declassify itself.

In the next section, we'll look at monitoring and managing policy matches.

Monitoring and managing DLP policy matches

From your DLP dashboard (`https://protection.office.com/insightdashboard`), you will be able to view many metrics in one place. You'll find three DLP-specific charts among them. If you select one of them, you will see the remaining two under **Related reports**. You can drill down into a selected chart to get more details regarding any matches, incidents, or false positives that appear.

Policy matches and incident reports are broken down by location (SharePoint, OneDrive, and so on). False positives and overrides are displayed by name. In the following screenshot, you can see the following information:

- Filter reports
- Export reports
- The ability to schedule the emails of reports (weekly or monthly):

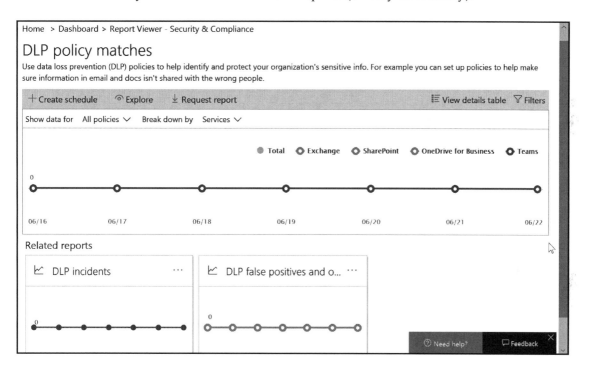

Note that, in order to view these reports, you must be a member of one of the following groups (with default settings applied). If you're not a member of one of these groups that include them, you must have one of the three roles indicated with * assigned to you:

- Exchange admin center:
    - Organization management group
    - Security reader group
    - Security reader role (automatically applied to members of the previous two groups)*
    - Compliance management group
    - View-only organization management group
    - View-only recipients (automatically applied to members of the previous two groups and the organization management group)*
- Security & Compliance Center:
    - Compliance administrator group
    - Organization management group
    - Security administrator group
    - Security reader group
    - View-only DLP compliance management role (automatically applied to members of the previous four groups)*

In the next and final section, we'll explore managing DLP exceptions in terms of policy triggers that should be ignored.

Managing DLP exceptions

When you start using DLP policy templates for the first time, it's likely that you'll run into situations where a high number of false positives come up, depending on the locale, as well as the data types you use frequently in your organization. In these situations, you can modify the DLP policies or create replacement policies to lessen the likelihood of locking people out or improperly retaining or deleting data.

If you're modifying a policy, you may consider adjusting the following properties:

- Confidence level (perhaps instead of 65%, you'll go with 80% confidence on credit card numbers)
- Sensitive data types and labels – perhaps a specific type of data is constantly being flagged but incorrectly
- The number of instances of a data type that's needed before a policy is triggered
- Override ability
- Policy tips
- Restrict (or not) content through encryption or permissions

You may find that a policy is being applied to a location that doesn't need it or, conversely, is missing from a location that needs it. To deal with this, modify an existing policy, or create a standalone policy, that will catch the other location.

 For the PowerShell pros out there, you can modify what constitutes a sensitive data type by following the instructions at `https://docs.microsoft.com/en-us/office365/securitycompliance/customize-a-built-in-sensitive-information-type`.

Summary

In this chapter, we covered the following MS-101 exam topics: how to configure DLP policies, designing data retention policies in Microsoft 365, monitoring and managing DLP policy matches, and managing DLP exceptions.

We started this chapter by configuring the DLP policies that are used in the Microsoft 365 Security & Compliance Center. You can use templates for data types that are protected by regulations such as HIPAA, or create custom policies that look for specific data types.

Then, you learned how to design data retention policies that protect data from being deleted before it's permitted to be by laws and regulations.

By completing this chapter, you can now manage and monitor any policy matches, as well as exceptions, from the DLP dashboard in the Microsoft 365 Security & Compliance Center (`https://protection.office.com/insightdashboard`).

In the next chapter, we'll look at implementing **Azure Information Protection** (**AIP**).

Questions

1. You need to ensure that the employees in your organization are only able to share documents that contain **personally identifiable information (PII)** with other employees in the organization, and block emails with PII being sent to anyone outside of it. You'll want to be able to share reports about emails that contain sensitive data. What should you configure?

   A. A retention policy in the Exchange admin center
   B. A retention policy in the Security & Compliance Center
   C. A **data loss prevention (DLP)** policy in the Exchange admin center
   D. A **data loss prevention (DLP)** policy in the Security & Compliance center

2. The following DLP policies are in place, and all of them apply to a recent incident. They are listed in their proper order/rank. Which rule's actions will be taken?

   Rule 1: Notifies user
   Rule 2: Notifies user, blocks user overrides, restricts access
   Rule 3: Notifies user, allows user overrides, restricts access
   Rule 4: Restricts access

   A. Rule 1 will be enacted
   B. Rule 2 will be enacted
   C. Rule 3 will be enacted
   D. Rule 4 will be enacted

Further reading

- **Configuring DLP policies**:
    - Getting started with DLP policy recommendations: `https://docs.microsoft.com/en-us/office365/securitycompliance/get-started-with-dlp-policy-recommendations`

- **Designing data retention policies in Microsoft 365**:
    - Overview of retention policies: `https://docs.microsoft.com/en-us/office365/securitycompliance/retention-policies`

- **Monitoring and managing DLP policy matches**:
    - Creating, testing, and tuning a DLP policy: `https://docs.microsoft.com/en-us/office365/securitycompliance/create-test-tune-dlp-policy`
- **Managing DLP exceptions**:
    - View reports for data loss prevention: `https://docs.microsoft.com/en-us/office365/securitycompliance/view-the-dlp-reports`
    - What the DLP functions look for: `https://docs.microsoft.com/en-us/office365/securitycompliance/what-the-dlp-functions-look-for`

10
Implementing Azure Information Protection (AIP)

Azure Information Protection (**AIP**) is a cloud-based solution that allows you to deploy clients to devices, implement policies, encrypt content, and configure services and users so that you can manage and protect your data. If you're familiar with Active Directory **Rights Management Services** (**RMS**), AIP offers all of the same familiar protection and features, with the added bonuses that are provided by it being a cloud-based solution.

In this chapter, we'll explore AIP in detail, looking specifically at the following MS-101 exam objectives:

- Planning an AIP solution
- Planning for classification labeling
- Deploying AIP clients
- Implementing an AIP tenant key
- Planning for **Windows Information Protection** (**WIP**) implementation
- Configuring **Information Rights Management** (**IRM**) for workloads
- Planning for the deployment of an on-premises Rights Management connector
- Implementing AIP policies
- Configuring a super user

Let's begin by planning our AIP solution.

Planning an AIP solution

AIP allows you to automatically or manually classify data for protection based on dedicated labels per data type. There are three ways labels can be applied to content (emails or documents):

- Automatically, by policy design (detects specified data types and applies labels accordingly)
- Manually, by users (selected from the available published labels in Exchange, SharePoint, or Office applications)
- Manually, by recommendation (if the AIP client has been deployed to devices, it will provide in-product notifications when sensitive data types are detected and suggest a label accordingly)

Your users could, for example, flag their own documents as confidential, which would apply a specific type of protection to the document. Alternatively, they could create a notice that appears at the top of a document-in-progress letting the user know it identified a social security number and suggests a certain label that can then be applied.

As an administrator, you can also plan AIP so that it automatically detects sensitive data types such as driver license numbers and applies a specific label to the email or document. The best solution, of course, would be a combination of manual options for user flexibility as well as automatic labels to make sure certain items are being caught.

AIP is not overly technical but is more about getting organized and implementing it in an effective way. In order to begin planning your AIP solution, you'll need to make sure you've already accomplished both of the following tasks:

- Users and groups are set up in Azure AD. You'll use these to create policies and manage permissions/roles.
- You are licensed for AIP so that you can give licenses to any individual who will be using AIP to classify and label data.

Once those prerequisite steps have been completed, you will complete the following steps to finish preparing for AIP:

1. Configure classification and labeling (see the next section, *Planning for classification labeling*).
2. Choose and deploy client(s) (see the *Deploying AIP clients* section in this chapter).
3. Install the PowerShell module for `AIPService` (formerly AADRM).

AADRM has been deprecated and replaced with the `AIPService` module. If you already have the AADRM module installed, uninstall it before installing the new `AIPService` module. You can find out more at `https://docs.microsoft.com/en-us/powershell/module/aadrm/?view=azureipps`.

In the next section, we'll plan classification labeling.

Planning for classification labeling

Out of the box, AIP comes with labels ready to use. You should customize these to suit your needs and add your own for employees to use. You'll find these in the AIP portal (`portal.azure.com` | search for `Azure Information Protection` | **Labels**). A best practice is to keep the number of labels you create and share with users to a minimum and to use language your users will understand intuitively as they assign the labels that are available to them to content.

As shown in the following screenshot, you can see **Label Display Name** (as a user will see it in their client and web applications) and each label's usage (in policy, just marking, or also protection).

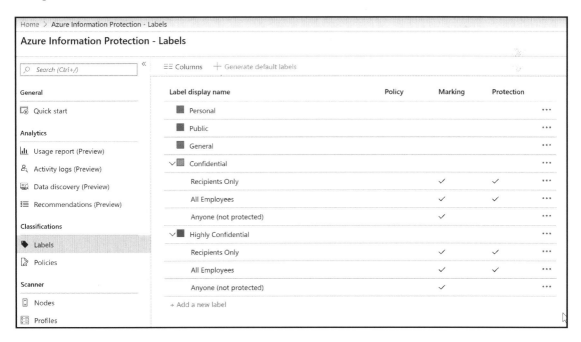

So, if we want to apply a **Do Not Forward** protection to the **Highly Confidential** label, we'd follow these steps:

1. Select the **Highly Confidential** label.
2. Under **Set permissions for documents and emails containing this label**, select **Protect** and make sure **Azure (cloud key)** is selected since it is the most appropriate option in this scenario:

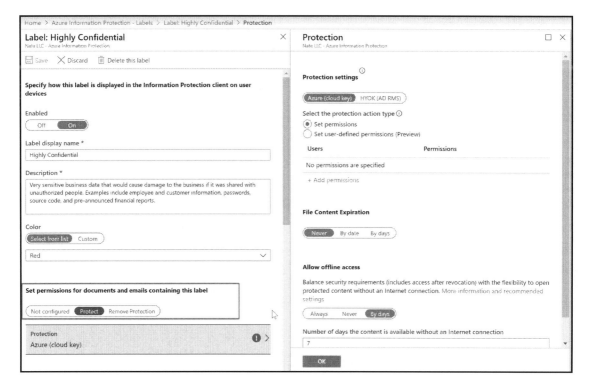

3. Change the protection action type radio button selection to **Set user-defined permissions (Preview).** Here, you'll notice that the **In Outlook apply Do Not Forward** box is already checked:

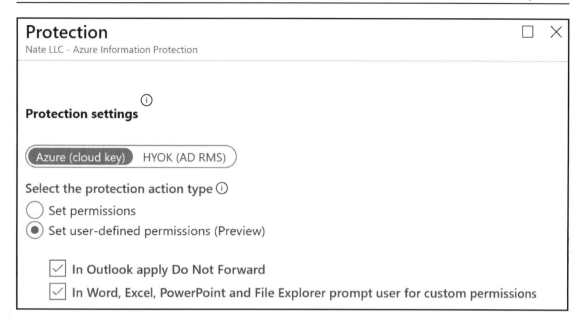

4. Click **OK** and then **Save**.

Now, let's look at deploying the AIP clients so that our users can benefit from in-product functionality.

Deploying AIP clients

AIP clients are deployed to machines to allow for increased coverage of our AIP solution. This is what allows in-product label recommendations, for example, when users are working with sensitive data in email messages or Office documents.

There are two AIP clients that you can deploy, both of which we'll cover in this section:

- Azure Information Protection client (classic)
- Azure Information Protection unified labeling client

The **classic client** downloads labels and information from Azure. The **unified labeling client** is more recent and incorporates labels and information from the following centers:

- Office 365 Security & Compliance (`protection.office.com`)
- Microsoft 365 Security Center (`security.microsoft.com`)
- Microsoft 365 Compliance Center (`compliance.microsoft.com`)

You may wish to use the classic client for advanced features such as an on-premises key **Hold-Your-Own-Key** (**HYOK**) or if you haven't migrated your labels to the unified labeling client yet.

However, the unified labeling client includes support for macOS, iOS, and Android devices, whereas the classic version doesn't. It will also receive new features going forward. It is recommended that you use the unified labeling client unless you need to use the classic client for a specific purpose.

 For a more in-depth dive into comparing the two clients, check out `https://docs.microsoft.com/en-us/azure/information-protection/rms-client/use-client`.

Installing either client is as simple as downloading and running an executable (`.exe`) or deploying a `.msi` file via Intune or group policy.

If you download the `.exe` file, you can install the client or unified labeling client in quiet mode by running `AzInfoProtection.exe /quiet` or `AzInfoProtection_UL.exe /quiet`, respectively.

Next, we'll implement the AIP tenant key.

Implementing an AIP tenant key

By default, Microsoft generates and manages your tenant key for you. This is the quickest and most cost-effective way to get started with AIP with the least amount of administrative effort and would be preferable for smaller organizations.

However, you may have compliance requirements that require you to manage your own tenant key. This is known as **Bring-Your-Own-Key** (**BYOK**). You could create the key in Azure Key Vault or in an on-premise HSM (which involves a monthly cost and Azure Key Vault Premium, where you'd import it).

A tenant key can be thought of as an umbrella that can cover/contain these *subkeys*:

- User keys
- Computer keys
- Document encryption keys

In the next section, we will plan for WIP.

Planning for WIP implementation

WIP is available for Windows 10 devices running version 1607 or later and can be managed through Intune, SCCM, or some third-party MDM solutions your company may be using.

WIP allows us to do the following:

- Allows users to use their personal devices to access company data without switching environments or apps
- Wipe devices while leaving personal data alone
- Track issues and remedial actions with audit reports
- Integrate with our MDM solution

An example scenario would be when data is downloaded via a device protected with WIP (such as from SharePoint to a removable USB drive). Here, the data will be encrypted on the device (the removable media, in this case). When the employee who downloaded the data leaves the company and they're removed, the encryption keys that they used to encrypt that data become invalid and attempting to open the file from the removable media will not work.

> You can learn how to create a WIP policy in Intune at `https://docs.`
> `microsoft.com/en-us/windows/security/information-protection/`
> `windows-information-protection/overview-create-wip-policy.`

Now, let's configure IRM.

Configuring IRM for workloads

Azure Rights Management Service (Azure RMS) is an **Information Rights Management (IRM)** solution that protects Office files across devices, even after they're downloaded from their sources, such as Exchange or SharePoint. The on-premise counterpart is the **Active Directory Rights Management Services (AD RMS)**.

Using the Rights Management connector (see the next section, *Planning for the deployment of the on-premises Rights Management connector*), you can make sure Exchange and SharePoint servers are benefiting from Azure RMS as well. And because it's a cloud-based service, there's no need to worry about configuring additional servers when considering scalability.

AIP for O365 is included in Office 365 E3 and E5 licenses. However, you'll need an AIP P1 or P2 license to use classification and labeling. AIP integrates with the following O365 services:

- Exchange online (automatically enabled in new tenants)
- SharePoint online
- OneDrive for Business

SharePoint and OneDrive IRM integration aren't automatic like Exchange, but you can enable it from a single setting. Within the SharePoint admin center, under **Settings | Classic**, you'll see a place for IRM. Just select **Use the IRM service...** and **Refresh IRM Settings**, as shown in the following screenshot:

Next, we'll plan the deployment of the on-premises Rights Management connector.

Planning for the deployment of an on-premises Rights Management connector

Cloud-based Microsoft RMS can utilize the on-premise IRM functionality by deploying the RMS connector. The connector can be installed on physical on-premises servers or **virtual machines** (**VMs**) running Windows 2008 R2 or later. You may install it, for example, on SharePoint and Exchange servers. Follow these steps:

1. Install the RMS connector.
2. Enter your credentials.
3. Authorize the servers so that they can use the RMS connector.
4. Configure load balancing and high availability.
5. Configure the servers so that they can use the RMS connector.

 You can follow the more detailed steps of the process at `https://docs.microsoft.com/en-us/azure/information-protection/install-configure-rms-connector`.

Now, we're ready to implement AIP policies.

Implementing AIP policies

Previously in this chapter, we discussed deploying the AIP clients. Once that's done, the policy you create can be downloaded to those clients. The policy may apply a default label to Exchange items and Office files, or it may just make the labels available to users to classify their content.

Here's an example of a modified global policy. You could just modify the global policy that applies to everyone, like this one, or create additional policies that apply to specific users and groups:

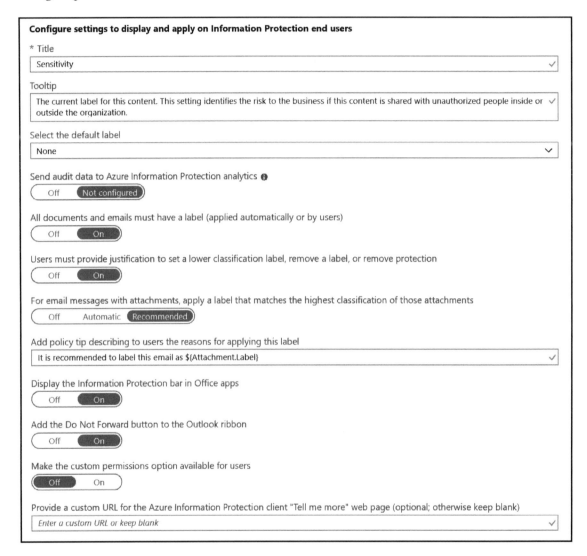

Configure settings to display and apply on Information Protection end users

* Title

Sensitivity

Tooltip

The current label for this content. This setting identifies the risk to the business if this content is shared with unauthorized people inside or outside the organization.

Select the default label

None

Send audit data to Azure Information Protection analytics

Off Not configured

All documents and emails must have a label (applied automatically or by users)

Off On

Users must provide justification to set a lower classification label, remove a label, or remove protection

Off On

For email messages with attachments, apply a label that matches the highest classification of those attachments

Off Automatic Recommended

Add policy tip describing to users the reasons for applying this label

It is recommended to label this email as ${Attachment.Label}

Display the Information Protection bar in Office apps

Off On

Add the Do Not Forward button to the Outlook ribbon

Off On

Make the custom permissions option available for users

Off On

Provide a custom URL for the Azure Information Protection client "Tell me more" web page (optional; otherwise keep blank)

Enter a custom URL or keep blank

Taken note of some of the powerful options here:

- Display the Information Protection bar in Office apps
- Add the **Do Not Forward** button to the Outlook ribbon
- Customizable policy tips for emails
- Require justification for lowering classification or removing protection

To get started, go to Azure (`portal.azure.com`), find the **Azure Information Protection** blade, and select **Policies**. From here, you can select the default **Global** policy or click **Add a new policy**:

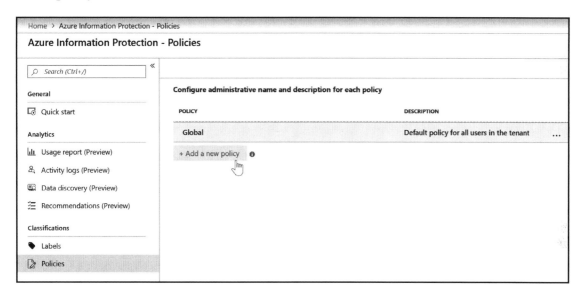

Next, let's find out what a super user is and how to configure one.

Configuring a super user

Super users can read and inspect data that's protected by Azure RMS in case of an emergency or the need for recovery. However, the super users feature is not enabled by default. You can enable it and assign super users by utilizing PowerShell:

1. Enable the super user feature:

```
Enable-AadrmSuperUserFeature
```

2. Assign a super user (this could be an individual or a service account):

```
Add-AadrmSuperUser -EmailAddress "NateCh@contoso.com"
```

Alternatively, you can use the following command:

```
Add-AadrmSuperUser -ServicePrincipalId
"1A234567-89B0-1234-5678-9C012345D67"
```

Alternatively, set a group as super users:

```
Set-AadrmSuperUserGroup -GroupEmailAddress "admin@contoso.com"
```

3. You can have the feature enabled when it's needed and then use the following cmdlet to disable it when it's not needed:

```
Disable-AadrmSuperUserFeature
```

If you're unsure who is already a super user or group, you can use `Get-AadrmSuperUser` or `Get-AadrmSuperUserGroup`, respectively.

Summary

In this chapter, we covered the exam topics that we outlined at the beginning of this chapter.

We learned that Azure AIP helps us protect sensitive data types from creation to storage and sharing using labels and protection template administrator controls. We created a label and applied protection to items using that label. To help users protect data when they're working in client applications, we deployed AIP clients to our user's devices. We learned that we can incorporate WIP and IRM into our overall information protection solution.

Then, we created and implemented AIP policies, which is the configuration that actually allows much of the functionality we discussed in this chapter, such as the notification bar in client applications. We ended this chapter by enabling a super user, that is, someone who can read and inspect data protected by Azure RMS.

In the next chapter, we'll explore managing data governance in our tenant.

Questions

1. You want users to be able to reclassify emails or documents as less sensitive than what they're automatically labeled, if appropriate. What must you configure to require submission of justification when changing an item's classification?

   A. Azure Information Protection - Label
   B. A retention policy in Security & Compliance
   C. A DLP policy in Security & Compliance
   D. An AIP policy

2. What must you configure to make sure users who have downloaded company data to USB drives are unable to access it once they've left the company?

   A. An AIP policy
   B. A WIP
   C. An Azure AD Identity Protection policy
   D. MDM authority

Further reading

- **Planning an Azure Information Protection (AIP) solution**:
    - *Azure Information Protection deployment roadmap*: https://docs.microsoft.com/en-us/azure/information-protection/deployment-roadmap
    - *Azure Information Protection overview*: https://azure.microsoft.com/en-us/services/information-protection/
- **Planning for classification labeling**:
    - *Quickstart: Configure a label for users to easily protect emails that contain sensitive information*: https://docs.microsoft.com/en-us/azure/information-protection/quickstart-label-dnf-protectedemail

- **Deploying AIP clients**:
    - *Azure Information Protection client: Installation and configuration for clients*: `https://docs.microsoft.com/en-us/azure/information-protection/configure-client`
    - *The client side of Azure Information Protection*: `https://docs.microsoft.com/en-us/azure/information-protection/rms-client/use-client`

- **Implementing AIP tenant key**:
    - *Planning and implementing your Azure Information Protection tenant key*: `https://docs.microsoft.com/en-us/azure/information-protection/plan-implement-tenant-key`

- **Planning for Windows Information Protection (WIP) implementation**:
    - *Create a Windows Information Protection (WIP) policy using Microsoft Intune*: `https://docs.microsoft.com/en-us/windows/security/information-protection/windows-information-protection/overview-create-wip-policy`

- **Configuring Information Rights Management (IRM) for workloads**:
    - *Comparing Azure Information Protection and AD RMS*: `https://docs.microsoft.com/en-us/azure/information-protection/compare-on-premise`

- **Planning for deployment of the on-premises Rights Management connector**:
    - *Deploying the Azure Rights Management connector*: `https://docs.microsoft.com/en-us/azure/information-protection/deploy-rms-connector`
    - *Installing and configuring the Azure Rights Management connector*: `https://docs.microsoft.com/en-us/azure/information-protection/install-configure-rms-connector`

- **Implementing AIP policies**:
    - *Configuring the Azure Information Protection policy*: `https://docs.microsoft.com/en-us/azure/information-protection/configure-policy`

- **Configuring a super user**:
    - *Configuring super users for Azure Rights Management and discovery services or data recovery*: `https://docs.microsoft.com/en-us/azure/information-protection/configure-super-users`

11
Managing Data Governance

A major part of designing your organization's data governance plan in Microsoft 365 is understanding the default retention and deletion actions that are implemented on the content of the various apps and services being utilized by your users. Some of these can be modified, and you can design custom retention policies to accurately reflect the unique needs of your organization and the industry regulations it may be subject to.

In this chapter, you will learn what tools are available for automating retention based on specified criteria, backing up your data, and working from backups to restore important data. This chapter will prepare you for the following exam topics:

- Planning and configuring information retention
- Planning for a Microsoft 365 backup
- Planning for restoring deleted content

Let's begin with planning and configuring information retention.

Planning and configuring information retention

We discussed designing retention policies in Microsoft 365 in `Chapter 9`, *Configuring Data Loss Prevention (DLP)*. Retention policies should be a central part of your data governance strategy and can involve deletion (automatic or allowed) as well. In this section, we'll take a closer look at creating a retention policy from the Microsoft 356 Compliance Center (`compliance.microsoft.com`).

Let's begin by looking at retention periods and possible deletion options once a retention period ends.

Retention period and deletion

When choosing a retention period, you can configure the period as follows:

- A period of time in years, months, or days
- Forever

You can base that time on an email's or document's date of creation or last modification. The following screenshot shows the retention policy creation wizard's screen for selecting a retention period:

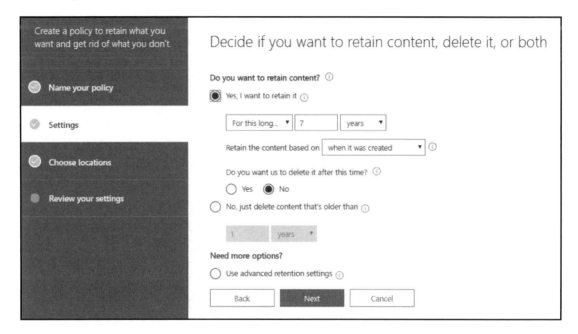

Note the option to automatically delete the content at the end of the retention period. Otherwise, the content remains and must be deleted manually. The policy will simply *allow* deletion after the retention period, whereas it's restricted during its active retention period.

You can also create a policy that just deletes content that is of a certain age, again based on creation or last modification. This would mean it *could* be deleted prior to that age by a user, but it ensures that content of a certain age or an inactive state is definitely deleted. This might be useful for content that is not subject to any industry regulations or laws but shouldn't be kept either because it could become a liability or because it simply clutters your digital environment.

Next, let's take a look at the apps and services that we can apply these retention policies to.

Locations

When configuring locations for a retention policy, you can choose from the following options:

- **All locations**: This includes content in Exchange email, Office 365 groups, OneDrive, and SharePoint documents.
- **Let me choose specific locations**: This allows you to get granular within each app and design separate policies for those specific apps as opposed to blanket policies for all (or nearly all) the apps in the tenant.

 Not all retention policy actions are available in all the apps and services. Note that, depending on your policy design on the **Settings** tab of the policy configuration wizard, some apps and services may not appear as options.

To help you in your policy design, the following list shows which actions are available for which apps and at what depth (all recipients or specific recipients, for example):

- Detect content that contains specific words or phrases:
    - **Exchange**: Include or exclude specific recipients
    - **SharePoint**: Include or exclude specific sites
    - **OneDrive**: Include or exclude specific OneDrive accounts
    - **O365 Groups**: Include or exclude specific groups
- Detect content that contains sensitive information (such as HIPAA or PII):
    - **SharePoint**: Include or exclude specific sites
    - **OneDrive**: Include or exclude specific OneDrive accounts
    - **Exchange email**: All
- There are regular retention settings (all content):
    - **Exchange email**: Include or exclude specific recipients
    - **SharePoint sites**: Include or exclude specific sites
    - **OneDrive accounts**: Include or exclude specific accounts
    - **Office 365 groups**: Include or exclude specific teams
    - **Skype for business (retained in Exchange)**: All or include specific users

- **Exchange public folders**: All
- **Teams channel messages**: Include or exclude specific teams
- **Teams chats**: Include or exclude specific users

Currently, if your policy applies specifically to Teams channel messages or chats, it cannot also apply to other apps. It must be a separate policy.

Note that you cannot include AND exclude within a location/app. Your condition must be inclusion OR exclusion. If nothing is selected, it includes **ALL** by default.

Creating a retention policy

Let's create a retention policy from scratch:

1. Go to the Microsoft 365 Compliance Center (compliance.microsoft.com).
2. Click on **Information governance | Retention**.
3. Click **+New retention policy**.
4. Name and describe your policy and click **Next**.
5. Choose whether you want your policy to apply to *all content* or for *specific content*. In this case, use the **Use advanced retention settings** option:

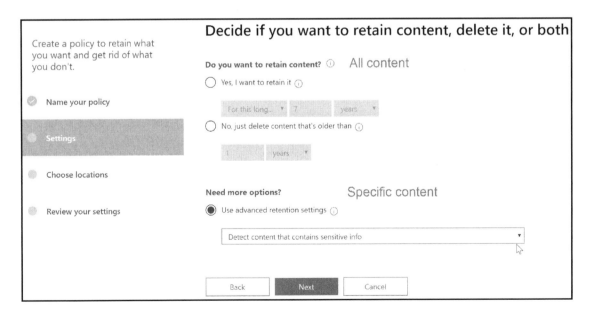

6. If you chose one of the first two options that apply to *all* content, skip to step 7. Otherwise, if you chose **Detect content that contains specific info** you'll choose from pre-built sensitive data type templates, just as we learned when creating **data loss prevention** (**DLP**) policies. But if you choose **Detect content that contains specific words or phrases**, you'll use a query box to enter keywords to search for within the content. This supports using OR, AND, and NOT as operators. In the future, this will also support using managed property searches such as department:Compliance or subject:Benefits. Once you've inserted your query text, select how long content that matches the query should be retained and which date property to use for duration (created, last modified, or when a label is applied):

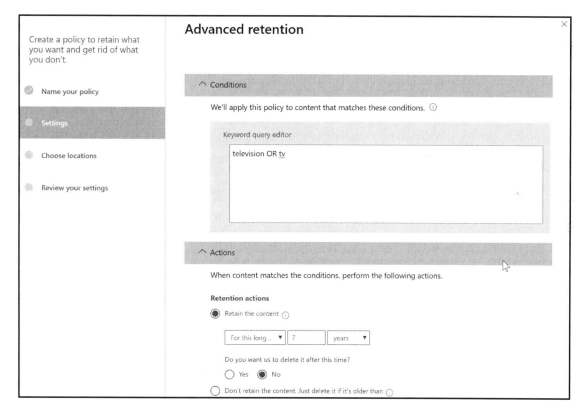

7. Choose the locations to include (SharePoint, Exchange, OneDrive, O365 Groups, and so on).

8. Review your settings and note that *it could take 7 days to begin applying retention policies* to items matching your policy. Now, do the following:
   1. Create the policy
   2. Save for later

In the next section, we'll switch focus from content retention to planning backups.

Planning for a Microsoft 365 backup

Before changing Office 365 for Business subscriptions for users, you'll want to back up their content to ensure nothing is lost. You may also wish to back up content for other purposes so that it can be restored or referenced in the event of a user error. Each app has different ways of accomplishing backups:

- For Outlook, you'll export a `.pst` file of the user's email, contacts, and calendar from the existing subscription and then import it into their new subscription.
- For OneDrive for Business documents, you can download their contents to a local drive or a different location (like you can do with SharePoint).
- In Yammer, admins can export all files, notes, messages, topics, users, and groups to a `.zip` file.
- SharePoint documents, such as OneDrive, can just be saved to another location. As for whole sites, as long as the user's new subscription is in the same organization, even if the new subscription doesn't have SharePoint Online, the user will still have access to SharePoint sites; the SharePoint icon just won't appear in their app launcher.

Now, content, backed up in its various ways, is recoverable should it be needed.

Note that, in SharePoint and OneDrive, versioning is available as another kind of backup at a granular level. If a user makes a mistake on a document, for example, or needs to compare versions, they can restore or just view previous versions of documents and pages using **Version history**.

Now that you know how to back up lots of content per app, let's take a look, at how we can restore specific mailboxes and individual content that's been deleted from within SharePoint and OneDrive.

Planning for restoring deleted content

A full backup isn't always what's best except in major restoration processes. Sometimes, you'll just need to restore individual files or sites. In this section, we'll cover the restoration process for content that's been deleted in Exchange, SharePoint, and OneDrive. We'll start with restoring mailboxes in Exchange.

Exchange

When a user leaves an organization and their user account is deleted, their mailbox is automatically retained and recoverable for 30 days. You would need to reactivate their user account to restore the mailbox.

If you place a retention policy or litigation hold on the user's mailbox *before* it is deleted, it can be retained beyond 30 days, making it an **inactive mailbox**. Retention policies in the Security & Compliance Center will only allow you to retain certain content matching a query or rules.

Inactive mailboxes can be **recovered** (for returning employees, this converts from being inactive into being active) or **restored** (this merges content into a new mailbox and preserves the inactive mailbox).

Now, let's explore our options for SharePoint.

SharePoint

In SharePoint Online, deleted items are kept for 93 days. If your users have deleted content, they can check the recycle bin on the site where they deleted it to before the end of the 93 days. If, during those 93 days, the item is deleted from the site's recycle bin (first-stage recycle bin), it will carry out its remaining days of the 93-day retention period in the site *collection* recycle bin (second-stage recycle bin). After 93 days have passed from its initial deletion date, or if the item is deleted from the second recycle bin, the item is permanently deleted.

You can restore deleted items from either recycle bin (site or site collection) as long as its original location still exists. If the original location, such as a document library, was deleted, you'd need to restore the library before you can restore the file.

To restore an item from a SharePoint site recycle bin, do the following:

1. Go to **Site settings** | **Site contents**.
2. Select **Recycle Bin** from the upper right-hand corner.
3. Select the item(s) to restore and click **Restore** from the ribbon menu.

As long as you're a site collection administrator, you'll see a link at the bottom of the site recycle bin to access the second-stage recycle bin to continue looking for a deleted item:

> Can't find what you're looking for? Check the Second-stage recycle bin

Restoring a document will restore all the versions associated with it when it was deleted and, similarly, restoring a list or library will restore with it all of the contents it held when it was deleted.

If a file has been deleted after its retention period in SharePoint Online, you can still contact Microsoft support within 14 days for assistance in getting it back.

If you delete an entire site collection, it can be restored from the SharePoint admin center by someone with sufficient permissions such as a global admin:

1. Go to the **SharePoint admin center**.
2. Click **Sites**.
3. Click **Deleted sites**.
4. Select the deleted site to restore.
5. Click on **Restore**.

Your deleted site will then be moved from **Deleted sites** to **Active sites** in the admin center:

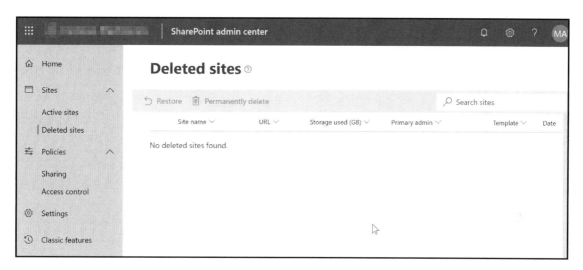

So far, we've seen how we can restore individual files or entire sites. There's a relatively newer feature called **Files Restore**, which allows us to *restore* a specific O365 document library to an earlier point in time (affects all the content in the library). The following screenshot shows us how to access this feature by selecting the settings wheel from the upper-right corner and then clicking **Restore this library**:

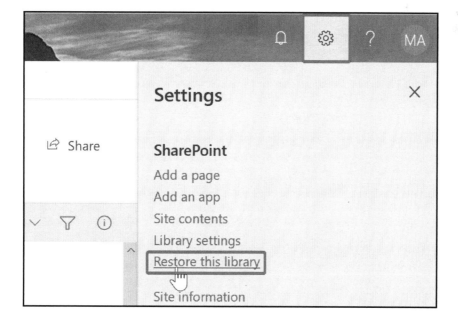

Once selected, you're able to choose a specific date and time, or even a specific change made to a particular document. Any changes made after that selected time/change will be undone, restoring the library its state before that time/change. The following screenshot shows specific document updates were used to select the point in time to which we'll be restoring the library.

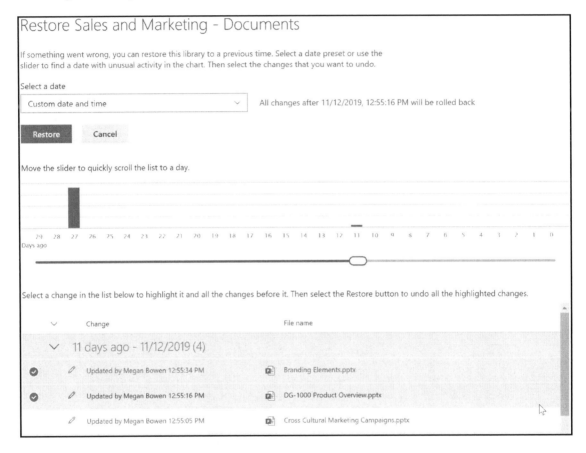

Files Restore is also available in OneDrive, which we'll cover next.

OneDrive

Every individual's OneDrive has a recycle bin, similar to SharePoint sites. The restoration process is the same in that you select the file(s) then **Restore**.

A newer feature in OneDrive, as we discussed in the previous subsection on SharePoint restoration, is called **Files Restore** and it allows you to revert the entirety of a OneDrive site (personal or business) to another point in time. You must have an Office 365 subscription to use this feature.

In both versions (personal and business), you'll find the restoration option by going to **Settings** | **Restore your OneDrive**:

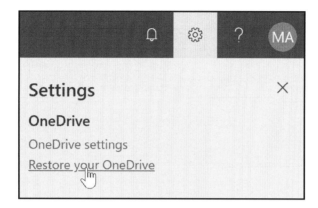

Then, you'll be able to use the dropdown menu, slider, or list of changes to choose the point in time that you wish to restore your OneDrive to:

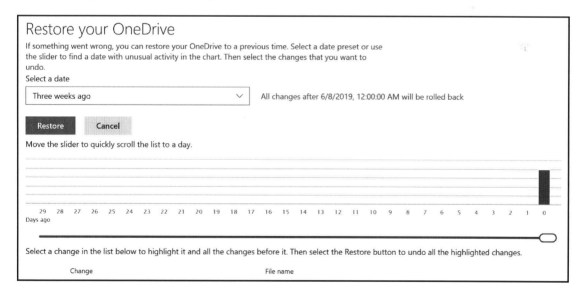

As you can see, we have many options for restoring content at a granular or global level. This provides peace of mind for users and should be documented in any existing retention and usage policies you may have.

Summary

In this chapter, we took a look at the data governance topics you'll find on the MS-101 exam, including the following:

- Plan and configure information retention
- Plan for Microsoft 365 backup
- Plan for restoring deleted content

First, we configured a retention policy and learned that it can apply to specific apps and services at a granular level. We know that we can create blanket policies (the same for many apps) or specifically targeted policies, such as actions to take for a Teams channel.

Then, we planned Microsoft 365 backups, learning specifically what our options were in Exchange, OneDrive for Business, Yammer, and SharePoint.

Finally, we took a look at where things go when they're deleted in Exchange, SharePoint, and OneDrive and how we can restore individual files, mailboxes, or entire sites or restore a library to a specific point in time using Files Restore.

In the next chapter, we'll look at the auditing capabilities in Microsoft 365.

Questions

1. What happens to content subject to the following retention policy once the retention period expires?

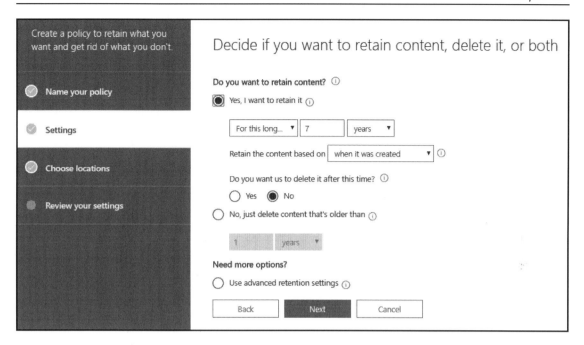

A. It is deleted.

B. The last modifier is emailed a notice, and the content is made read-only.

C. It moves to a records library but is not deleted.

D. It can be deleted but is not deleted automatically.

2. A user reports they've deleted a Power BI file from a SharePoint Online site's recycle bin by emptying the recycle bin and they need to get it back. The file was originally deleted 94 days ago. What can you do?

A. Restore it from the site's recycle bin.

B. Restore it from the site collection's second-stage recycle bin.

C. Contact Microsoft Support for assistance in restoring it.

D. Nothing—the file has passed its recovery window.

Further reading

- **Planning and configuring information retention**:
  - *Overview of retention policies*: https://docs.microsoft.com/en-us/ office365/securitycompliance/retention-policies

- **Planning for a Microsoft 365 backup**:
    - *Back up data before switching Office 365 for business plans*: `https://docs.microsoft.com/en-us/office365/admin/subscriptions-and-billing/back-up-data-before-switching-plans?view=o365-worldwide`
- **Planning for restoring deleted content**:
    - **Exchange**:
        - *Overview of inactive mailboxes in Office 365*: `https://docs.microsoft.com/en-us/office365/securitycompliance/inactive-mailboxes-in-office-365`
        - *Restore an inactive mailbox in Office 365*: `https://docs.microsoft.com/en-us/office365/securitycompliance/restore-an-inactive-mailbox`
        - *Recover an inactive mailbox in Office 365*: `https://docs.microsoft.com/en-us/office365/securitycompliance/recover-an-inactive-mailbox`
    - **SharePoint**:
        - *Restore items in the Recycle Bin of a SharePoint site*: `https://support.office.com/en-us/article/restore-items-in-the-recycle-bin-of-a-sharepoint-site-6df466b6-55f2-4898-8d6e-c0dff851a0be`
        - *Restore deleted items from the site collection recycle bin*: `https://support.office.com/en-us/article/restore-deleted-items-from-the-site-collection-recycle-bin-5fa924ee-16d7-487b-9a0a-021b9062d14b`
        - *Restore deleted sites*: `https://docs.microsoft.com/en-us/sharepoint/restore-deleted-site-collection`
    - **OneDrive**:
        - *Restore your OneDrive*: `https://support.office.com/en-us/article/restore-your-onedrive-fa231298-759d-41cf-bcd0-25ac53eb8a15`

12
Managing Auditing

Audit logs allow us, as administrators, the ability to find specific actions done by specific people in any or all applications in our tenant.

In this chapter, we'll take a look at the tools available for configuring audit logs and policies. While this chapter is short, it will cover basic abilities in auditing that are likely to appear on the exam:

- Configuring audit log retention
- Configuring the audit policy
- Monitoring unified audit logs
- Azure AD audit and sign-in logs

Let's begin with configuring audit log retention.

Configuring audit log retention

Audit logging keeps track of all sorts of actions that users are taking in your environment across various apps and services. You might find actions included as significant as adding someone to an owner's group with full permission or as small as modifying a document.

Audit logging is not turned on by default, so an administrator will need to turn it on before your organization can benefit from it. The least permissive way of granting this level of authority is to **provide the Audit Logs role in Exchange Online** (not Security & Compliance). If someone just needs to view/search the logs, they could be assigned the **View-Only Audit Logs** role. The following screenshot shows a custom admin role group being created and both **Audit Logs** and **View-Only Audit Logs** are selected. In reality, you'd select one or the other (not both):

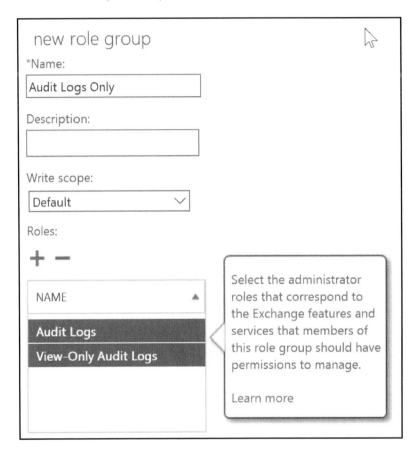

To turn it on, an admin with appropriate privileges (the **Audit Logs** role) can go to the Office 365 Security & Compliance Center (`protection.office.com`) | **Search** | **Audit log search** | **Start recording user and admin activities**:

The audit log will then capture any actions going forward but, of course, will not be able to provide historical actions that took place before the start of recording. Within a couple of hours of starting recording, you will be able to begin searching the audit log for specific activity and users.

Another method of activating the audit log is through Exchange Online PowerShell:

```
Set-AdminAuditLogConfig -UnifiedAuditLogIngestionEnabled $true
```

The only way to turn *off* audit logging is via PowerShell, in which you'll use the same command as the preceding, but change `$true` to `$false`.

Audit logging can capture ~500 activity types from the following categories (with examples). Take some time to get a good understanding of the activities in this list in case they appear in a scenario on the exam:

- File and page (accessed, downloaded, or deleted)
- Folder (created, restored, or deleted)
- SharePoint list (updated item, created column, or created content type)
- Sharing and access request (accepted access request, created anonymous link, or added a permission level)
- Synchronization (downloaded or synced files to computer, or uploaded files)

- Site permission (created group, broke sharing inheritance, or modified permission level)
- Site administration (registered hub site, allowed user to create groups, or renamed site)
- Exchange mailbox (added delegate permissions, used send on behalf of permissions, or deleted items)
- Sway (created, shared, deleted, or turned on external sharing)
- User administration (added user, changed license, or changed or reset password)
- Azure AD group administration (added, updated, or deleted)
- Application administration (added, set, or removed delegation entry)
- Role administration (added or removed member from role)
- Directory administration (added domain, turned on Azure AD sync, or set company information)
- eDiscovery (started content search, purged results, or removed search report)
- eDiscovery cmdlet (created, shared, or deleted search or deleted hold)
- Advanced eDiscovery (tag created, export run, or document downloaded)
- Power BI (created, published, viewed, edited, printed, or deleted)
- Microsoft Workplace Analytics (updated settings or partitions)
- Microsoft Teams (created team, added channel, or added connector)
- Dynamics 365 (signed in, activated process or plug-in, or performed bulk actions)
- Microsoft Flow (created, deleted, or edited permissions)
- PowerApps app (created, published, or edited permissions)
- Microsoft Stream video (created, edited, or shared)
- Microsoft Stream group channel (created, edited, or deleted groups or channels)
- Microsoft Stream general (edited or deleted users or edited global role members)
- LabelExplorer (accessed item)

All of the preceding audit log activity examples are included as searchable activities by default. However, SharePoint site activities and Exchange mailbox activities will not return results until you've done additional configuration in each of those services.

Let's look at how to enable the auditing of SharePoint site activities.

Enabling auditing of SharePoint site activities

As mentioned, SharePoint site activities aren't captured by default. You'll need to follow these steps to make sure a site's activity is included in the audit logs:

 Enabling auditing of SharePoint site activities may appear on the exam. However, in the future, audit experiences in SharePoint will be powered by the Unified Audit pipeline which will replace trimming and choosing specific events to audit per site collection as described here.

1. Go to **Site Settings** (**Settings** | **Site Settings** for the classic experience, and **Settings** | **Site information** | **View all site settings** for the modern experience).
2. Click on **Site collection audit settings** under **Site Collection Administration**.
3. Check boxes for each activity you want to monitor (editing items, deleting items, editing permissions, and so on) and click **OK** to save:

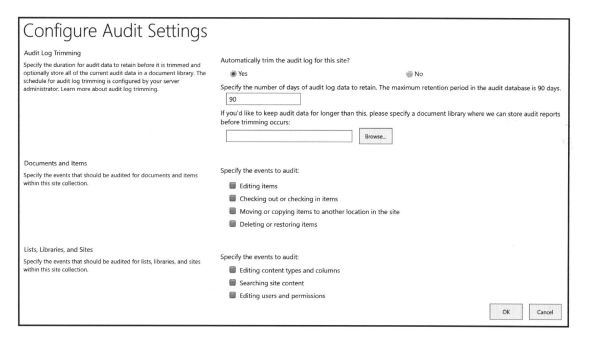

4. Repeat this for each site collection you want included in the audit logs.

Now, let's see how to enable Exchange mailbox activity audits.

Enabling auditing of Exchange mailbox activities

Similar to SharePoint, we need to enable auditing of Exchange mailboxes before their activities will appear in the audit log. We can do this for all users or specific users using one of the following PowerShell commands:

1. Run the following Exchange Online PowerShell command to enable auditing at the mailbox level for a **single user**:

   ```
   Set-Mailbox 'Nate Chamberlain' -AuditEnabled $true
   ```

2. Run the following command to enable auditing for **all users**:

   ```
   Get-Mailbox -ResultSize Unlimited -Filter {RecipientTypeDetails -
   eq "UserMailbox"} | Set-Mailbox -AuditEnabled $true
   ```

In the next section, we'll configure audit policies.

Configuring the audit policy

One of the exam skills is configuring the audit policy, but it was made part of the exam's skill listing before some of the newer Office 365 features were available. There really isn't a lot to configure, as much of the auditing is enabled by default now (see the list of activity examples in the previous section). That being said, it's still helpful to be aware of the following information.

With an Office 365 E3 license, you're given 90 days of audit log retention. Office 365 E5 licenses get 365 days OR you can purchase the Office 365 Advanced Compliance add-on (currently in a package called **Information Protection & Compliance**), which would also grant 365 days' auditing.

As seen in the last section's screenshot for enabling auditing in SharePoint, you could choose specifically in a SharePoint site collection, to keep fewer days or to extend beyond the 90 days by utilizing a document library for storage of the logs.

The audit log you've enabled is unified, meaning Microsoft has consolidated audit log abilities that were once separated across the various apps and services. This is why, currently, selecting **Audit logs** from the Power BI admin portal will redirect you to the Office 365 Admin Center. We'll discuss the unified audit log more in the following section:

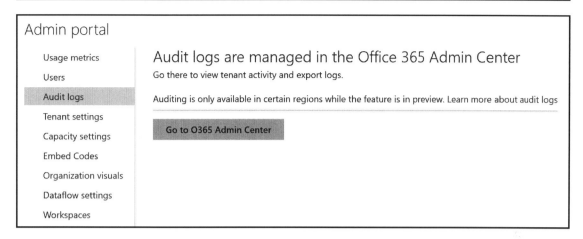

Now, let's see how we can monitor the unified audit logs.

Monitoring unified audit logs

The unified audit log (`protection.office.com/unifiedauditlog`) is where users with the Exchange Online **View-Only Audit Logs** or **Audit Logs** role (granted by default to users with the Compliance Management, Organization Management, or Global admin roles) can view and search activity logs collected across Microsoft 365:

1. Go to **Audit Logs** (Office 365 Security & Compliance | **Search** | **Audit log search**).
2. Select **Activities** (there are around 500 to choose from).
3. Select the beginning and end dates and times to include.
4. Select **Users** or leave it blank for all users.
5. If you are narrowing to a specific filename or folders with a keyword, you can enter that.
6. Click **Search** to return results, or you can use your configured search to create an alert policy.

7. If you run a search, you can then filter results further by any of the column headers or export the results as a CSV file:

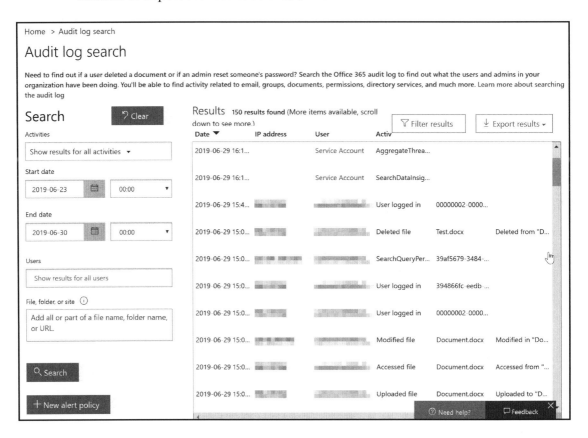

As you can see, it's easy to get custom reports and find exact details for certain events, and, with the alert policy option, we can make sure we're notified instead of needing to comb over the report regularly.

In the last section, let's take a brief look at the audit and sign-in logs provided by Azure AD.

Azure AD audit and sign-in logs

In Azure AD (`portal.azure.com` | **Azure Active Directory**) under **Monitoring**, you'll find **Sign-ins** and **Audit logs** available:

Sign-ins will show you user sign-in attempts, app usage, sign-in physical locations, and whether MFA or conditional access was utilized to sign them in.

Audit logs provide a wealth of activity logging for all changes in Azure AD including inviting users, group membership or user role changes, password updates, or policy assignments.

Summary

In this chapter, we reviewed the possibilities for capturing and monitoring audit logs for Microsoft 365 apps and services.

We configured retention by starting data collection as an administrator with at least the Audit Logs role. We then had to enable audit log activity tracking for SharePoint sites and Exchange mailboxes separately.

We learned most of our auditing is enabled by default, and that E3 licenses give us 90 days' logging, and E5 licenses give us 365 days' worth.

We looked at the unified audit log and found that we have lots of flexibility in searching for, and filtering to, specific content across our tenant and that we can create alert policies for specific activities that appear.

We learned that Azure AD also has sign-in activity and audit logs available.

In the next and final chapter before the mock exams and assessment, we'll learn about eDiscovery.

Questions

1. The HR Director asks you to provide a report of all sharing, copying, downloading, and so on, that's happened with a file from the HR site collection called `TalentAcquisition.xlsx`. What should you use to get the report to them in the most restrictive way with the least amount of administrative effort?

   A. Audit log search export
   B. Add HR Director to a group with the Compliance Management role
   C. Azure Information Protection activity log export
   D. Azure AD audit logs export

2. You need to allow a compliance manager to view and search the audit log, but not run cmdlets against it (such as turning off auditing). What role should you assign to this user in the Exchange admin center?

   A. Audit Log Manager
   B. Read-Only Audit Logs
   C. Audit Logs
   D. View-Only Audit Logs

Further reading

- **Configure audit log retention**:
    - *Turn Office 365 audit log search on or off*: https://docs.microsoft.com/en-us/office365/securitycompliance/turn-audit-log-search-on-or-off

    - *Permissions in Exchange Online*: https://docs.microsoft.com/en-us/Exchange/permissions-exo/permissions-exo

- **Configure audit policy**:
    - *Configure your Office 365 tenant for increased security*: https://docs.microsoft.com/en-us/office365/securitycompliance/tenant-wide-setup-for-increased-security

    - *Manage mailbox auditing*: https://docs.microsoft.com/en-us/office365/securitycompliance/enable-mailbox-auditing/

- **Monitor Unified Audit Logs**:
  - *Search the audit log in the Security & Compliance Center*: `https://docs.microsoft.com/en-us/office365/security compliance/search-the-audit-log-in-security-and-compliance`

13
Managing eDiscovery

When it comes to legal holds and compliance, Microsoft 365 has you covered. In this chapter, you'll explore the Security & Compliance Center (`protection.office.com`) and see how you can configure eDiscovery settings and features to enhance your organization's ability to mitigate and respond to issues.

To be able to use the Security & Compliance Center's eDiscovery features, you'll need to be a member of one of the following role groups:

- Compliance Administrator (case management, compliance search, and holds)
- eDiscovery manager and administrator (most permissive, includes all eDiscovery roles except search and purge)
- Organization management (same as Compliance Administrator, but adds search and purge role)
- Reviewer (review things assigned to them but can't open, create, or manage eDiscovery cases)

Specifically, in this chapter, we'll cover the following exam topics:

- Searching content using the Security & Compliance Center
- Planning for in-place and legal holds
- Configuring eDiscovery

Let's begin by learning about the *search content* feature of the Security & Compliance Center.

Searching content using the Security & Compliance Center

The Office 365 Security & Compliance Center allows you to search content across many locations in Microsoft 365 using a single search. The search is an essential part of eDiscovery cases, providing a starting place for discovering content matching specific criteria. We'll be covering cases in the *Configuring eDiscovery* section.

When setting up a *new* search, you have two options:

- **New search** (normal search setup)
- **Guided search** (wizard-guided setup)

Once you've completed a new search, you can export its export file to run a search based on its ID list by selecting **Search by ID List**. This requires you to upload a previous search's export file to narrow a new search to specific items within the export file.

The following screenshot shows the start of configuring a new search and the three aforementioned options:

The first two options (**New search** and **Guided search**) are the same in respect of configuration options; it's just a matter of user experience preference. The third (**Search by ID List**) might be useful if you need to check to see whether specific users or items came up matching your search conditions, such as seeing whether a specific user emailed another specific user during a certain time period.

When beginning a new search, you can choose to search all locations listed in the screenshot that follows or choose specifically among them. These locations include apps and services in which you can then narrow down your search to specific items such as the following:

- Users, groups, or teams
- SharePoint/Teams/OneDrive sites

Check out the following screenshot:

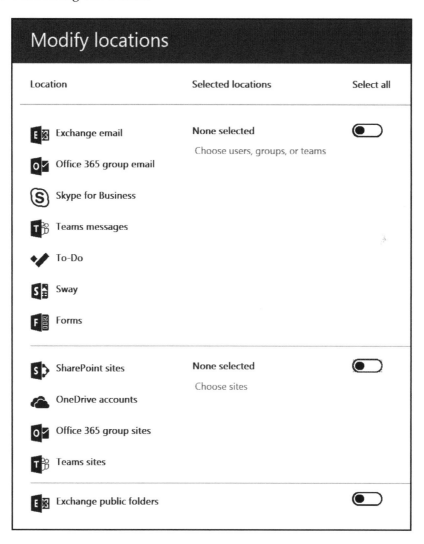

Note that you're unable to select individual Exchange public folders. The location, if selected, will include *all* Exchange public folders. The same applies to placing holds, which we'll discuss later this chapter.

You can also narrow your search by several characteristics/conditions, including the following:

- **Common**: This includes the following:
    - Date
    - Sender/Author
    - Size (in bytes)
    - Subject/Title
    - Compliance Label
- **Email**: This includes the following:
    - Message kind
    - Participants
    - Type
    - Received
    - Recipients
    - Sender
    - Sent
    - Subject
    - To
- **Documents**: This includes the following:
    - Author
    - Title
    - Created
    - Last modified
    - File type

Here are the steps to search content across Microsoft 365 using the Office 365 Security & Compliance Center:

1. Go to the Security & Compliance Admin Center (protection.office.com).
2. Click **Search** | **Content Search**.
3. Click **+ New search**.
4. Add any keywords in the keyword box to search for, if applicable.
5. Add any conditions by using the **+ Add conditions** button.

6. Select specific locations or select **All locations**.
7. Click **Save & run**.

Because searches are saved, you can easily come back and run the same search again at a later time. You can also leave the search running while you navigate to other pages, then come back later to open the search and view or export results.

If you come back to view the results of a search later, you'll go to **Search | Content search** in the Security & Compliance Admin Center and select the name of the search you ran. A pane will open with **View results** and **More | Export Report** as options:

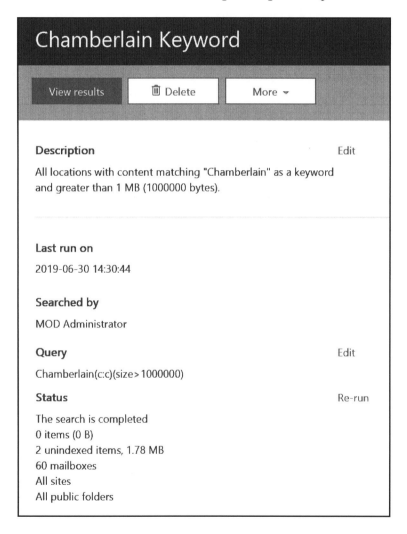

Even as a global admin, you may receive a message when viewing results that reads: **To preview search results, please ask your Compliance Admin to grant you Preview permission**. You'll need to ask the Compliance Admin to add the **Preview** role for you in **Permissions** or, if you're a global admin, add yourself. You can't modify default groups, so you may need to create a new group and assign the role and membership there:

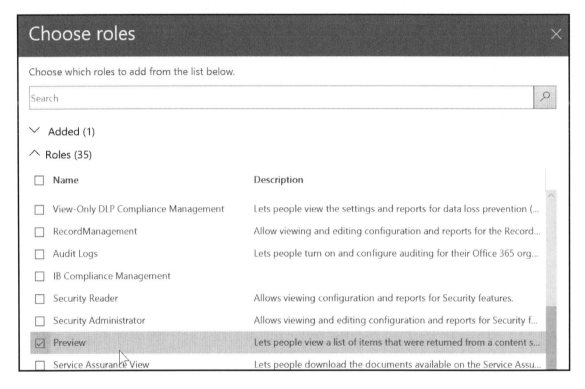

In the next section, we'll learn how to plan for in-place and legal holds.

Planning for in-place and legal holds

In-place and legal holds can be thought of as an extension of content search, where you'll be querying for specific content across multiple locations but then placing a hold on the results to preserve them for a period of time, whether indefinitely or with a set end date. These holds are usually due to protecting an organization in possible litigation scenarios in which failure to retain data relevant to a case might result in financial or legal risks to the organization.

In-place holds can be granular, using keywords or conditions to find specific content. **Litigation holds** can only be applied to *all* items. When configuring a hold, you'll want to know or consider the following:

- Content to be held and its location(s): If you're not holding **all** content, you'll also want to consider the following:
    - Keywords to find the content
    - Conditions/characteristics of items (sender, subject, last modified, and so on)
- Duration of hold, unless indefinite (or end date unknown)

Following are some notes to keep in mind for the exam:

- Holds on mailboxes apply to both the primary and archive mailboxes (even if in a hybrid deployment, the mailbox is on-premises and archive is in the cloud).
- Holds happen mostly in the background so users are unaffected.
- Holds are set up in a way that allow you to place multiple holds on a single user simultaneously. The combined holds cannot contain more than a total of 500 keywords between them, or the hold will auto-adjust to place **all** content on hold until the number of total keywords being queried is reduced.

Holds can be placed on a single mailbox or all mailboxes. To place a single mailbox on hold, you can use the Exchange Management Shell command that follows, where the duration is in days:

```
Set-Mailbox nchamberlain@contoso.com -LitigationHoldEnabled $true -
LitigationHoldDuration 365
```

When the hold can be removed (if prior to a specified duration), just change $true to $false in the preceding and remove the duration property.

Alternatively, you can place all mailboxes on litigation hold using the following:

```
Get-Mailbox -ResultSize Unlimited -Filter {RecipientTypeDetails -eq
"UserMailbox"} | Set-Mailbox -LitigationHoldEnabled $true -
LitigationHoldDuration 365
```

Note that duration is calculated from the received/created date for an individual item, and not from the date of initializing the hold.

Before you can begin a hold, you must have first created an eDiscovery case the hold is associated with:

1. Open the eDiscovery case you're working with.
2. Click **Holds** then **+ Create**.
3. Work through the wizard, very similar to the content search setup, and click **Create this hold**. Note that it could take an hour or so to take effect:

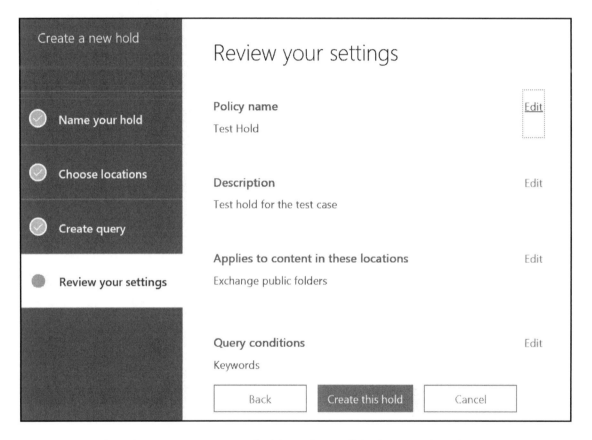

4. Back in the eDiscovery case dashboard, you'll find it now listed under **Holds** and you can, at any time, select it to see a side panel with statistics with the option to end or edit the hold:

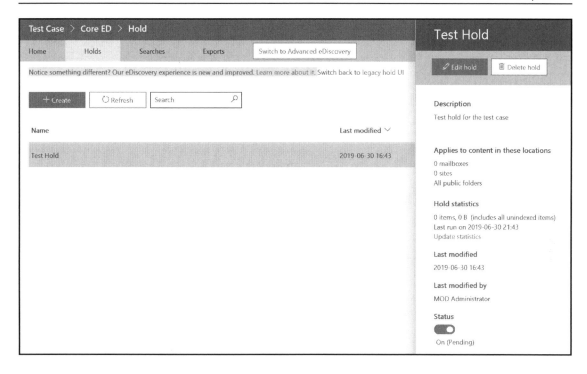

Next, let's configure eDiscovery.

Configuring eDiscovery

eDiscovery cases help to consolidate searches, holds, and general statistics on an eDiscovery event. They're useful in permissions, particularly, because you can have eDiscovery administrators (access to all eDiscovery cases) and eDiscovery managers (access to just their own cases). This keeps separate cases and their associated activity confidential except to those who must see all.

Note that not all eDiscovery cases have to have holds. An eDiscovery case can be created just for an eDiscovery manager to be able to perform and analyze content searches.

When creating a case, you're going to see familiar steps, similar to what we've seen when configuring a search outside of a case:

1. Go to the Security & Compliance Center (`protection.office.com`).
2. Click on **eDiscovery** | **eDiscovery**.

3. Click + **Create a case**.

4. Name and describe your case and save it. Click **Open** next to its name once saved.

5. From here, you can create holds (exactly as seen in the last section, *Planning for in-place and legal holds*) or perform searches (as seen in this chapter's first section, *Searching content using the Security & Compliance Center*). These activities are saved within an accessible location to those with access to the case, which acts as a container for all relevant activities.

Now that you know how to create cases, your compliance managers can have multiple cases they monitor simultaneously while keeping all relevant information in one location.

Summary

In this chapter, we covered the following exam topics:

- Search content using the Security & Compliance Center
- Planning for in-place and legal holds
- Configuring eDiscovery

We learned that we can search content across our tenant using the Security & Compliance Center (`protection.office.com`). We can, for example, find content modified or created by specific people during specific time spans with specific keywords. The granularity of these searches are nearly endless.

We planned for in-place and legal holds, knowing that it provides an option to lock content subject to an eDiscovery case in the event a user may try to modify or delete it before a case is closed.

We configured eDiscovery for our tenant, making it possible for compliance managers to create and review cases as needed. We know that the **Preview** role can be assigned to users needing to dissect the contents of any search.

This concludes the content chapters of this exam guide, covering every topic listed for the MS-101 exam. In the next two chapters, you'll find mock exams to help you to practice for the exams followed by a final *Assessment* section with answers and explanations to all chapter reviews and both mock exams.

Questions

1. Someone is trying to view the results of a content search in the Security & Compliance Center but when they click **View Results**, they get the following error message. They are not an administrator but should have access to preview content search results:

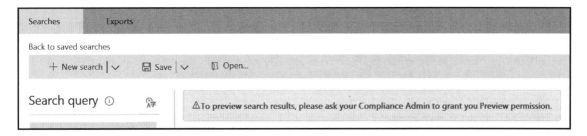

   How should you configure permissions in the most restrictive/minimal way so that they can view the results?

   A. Add them to a new or existing group with the **Preview** role assigned.
   B. Add them to the eDiscovery Administrator group.
   C. Add them to the eDiscovery Manager group.
   D. Add the Review role to the Security Reader group.

2. Your director asks for a report of all emails sent to George Blithe between 7/30 and 8/1 with the word *Phoenix* in it. You run a content search for that criteria from the Security & Compliance Center using **Guided search**. Does this meet the requirement?

   A. Yes
   B. No

Further reading

- **Searching content using the Security & Compliance Center**:
  - *Content Search in Office 365*: https://docs.microsoft.com/en-us/office365/securitycompliance/content-search
  - *Prepare a CSV file for an ID list Content Search in Office 365*: https://docs.microsoft.com/en-us/office365/securitycompliance/csv-file-for-an-id-list-content-search

- **Planning for in-place and legal holds**:
    - *In-Place Hold and Litigation Hold*: `https://docs.microsoft.com/en-us/exchange/security-and-compliance/in-place-and-litigation-holds`
    - *Place a mailbox on Litigation Hold*: `https://docs.microsoft.com/en-us/Exchange/policy-and-compliance/holds/litigation-holds`

- **Configuring eDiscovery**:
    - *eDiscovery cases in the Security & Compliance Center*: `https://docs.microsoft.com/en-us/office365/securitycompliance/ediscovery-cases`
    - *Assign eDiscovery permissions in the Security & Compliance Center*: `https://docs.microsoft.com/en-us/office365/securitycompliance/assign-ediscovery-permissions`

Section 4: Mock Exams

4

This section is all about assessing your knowledge of the content that we covered in *Sections 1-3*. You'll focus on preparing for the MS-101 exam by working through two mock exams (20 questions each).

This section includes the following chapters:

14
Mock Exam 1

1. The super user feature is disabled. Add Marlon Jackson
   (`marlon.jackson@contoso.com`) as a super user so he can read and inspect
   data protected by Azure RMS by choosing from the following commands for
   each line.
   (1)_____
   (2)_____
   (3)_____`"marlon.jackson@contoso.com"`

   - A. `Add-AadrmSuperUser`
   - B. `-EmailAddress`
   - C. `Set-AadrmSuperUser`
   - D. `-UserIdentifier`
   - E. `Enable-AadrmSuperUser`
   - F. `Enable-AadrmSuperUserFeature`

2. You piloted 25 devices with Microsoft Defender ATP, storing data in Europe. The
   pilot period has concluded, but you need to relocate the data to the United States.
   What should you do?

   - A. Offboard the pilot devices.
   - B. Open a ticket with Microsoft.
   - C. Delete the workspace in Azure.
   - D. Create a new workspace in Azure.

3. Emails with `#secure` in the subject line need to be encrypted. What should you
   do?

   - A. Create a message trace in the O365 Security & Compliance Center.
   - B. Modify the default AIP policy.
   - C. Create a message trace in the Exchange admin center.
   - D. Create a mail flow rule in the Exchange admin center.

4. The following screenshot shows the trigger conditions for a data loss prevention policy that applies to SharePoint document libraries:

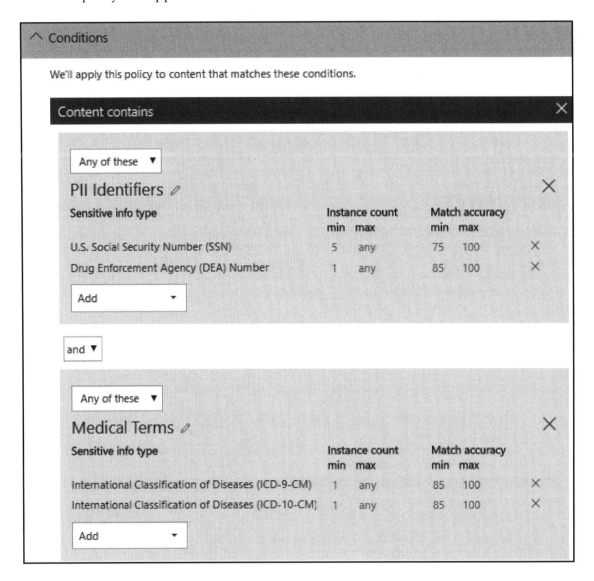

A document with **5 U.S. Social Security Numbers** is uploaded to a document library. Does this trigger the policy?

    A. Yes
    B. No

5. Your Azure AD Identity Protection Dashboard shows a sign-in from an unfamiliar location. What should you create to require multi-factor authentication from unfamiliar locations?

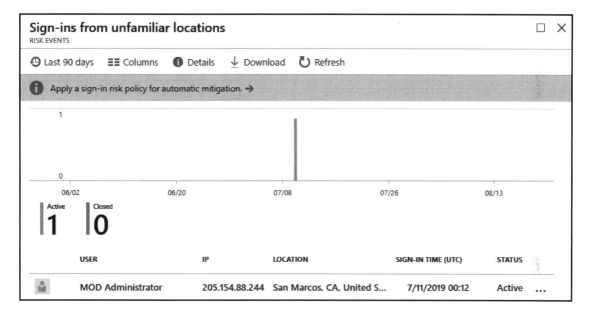

    A. Named location in Azure AD
    B. User risk policy
    C. Data loss prevention policy
    D. Sign-in risk policy

6. You're creating a data loss prevention policy that prevents HIPAA-protected information from leaving the organization. However, you need to make sure a partner organization can still receive this information, even though they're using a different domain. The policy's actions are configured as seen in the following screenshot. What else must you configure to allow **Company B** to continue to receive protected information?

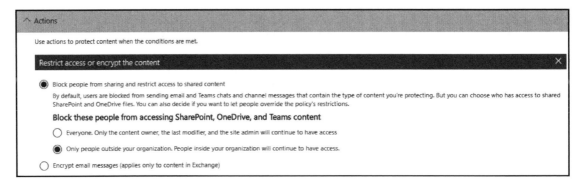

    A. Create a user risk policy in Azure AD.
    B. Create a named location in Azure AD.
    C. Modify the DLP policy's exceptions.
    D. Modify the DLP policy's conditions.

7. A member of your organization's compliance team needs to be able to place a hold on mailbox content. Which role should they be assigned?

    A. Compliance data administrator from Azure AD
    B. Exchange admin from the Microsoft 365 admin center
    C. eDiscovery Manager from the Security & Compliance Center
    D. Compliance management in the Exchange admin center

8. The next three questions will deal with the following screenshot and the topic of anti-phishing policies. Imagine you've configured the following anti-phishing policy in the Security & Compliance Center:

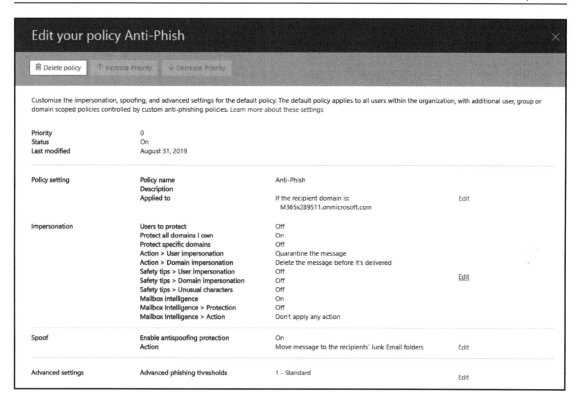

What will happen if the policy detects domain impersonation in a message?

    A. The message is moved to deleted items.

    B. The message is sent to quarantine.

    C. The message is sent with a warning tip.

    D. No action is applied.

9. In the same anti-phishing policy seen in *Question 8*, what will happen if the policy detects user impersonation in a message?

    A. The message is moved to deleted items.

    B. The message is sent to quarantine.

    C. The message is sent with a warning tip.

    D. No action is applied

10. You need to reduce the likelihood of an anti-phishing impersonation policy generating false positives. You configure mailbox intelligence. Does this meet the requirement?

    A. Yes
    B. No

11. By following the principle of least privilege, you need to assign someone who needs to be able to read and inspect data protected by Azure Rights Management. You enable the super user feature using PowerShell and assign that role to them. Does this meet the requirement?

    A. Yes
    B. No

12. Which type of device is more common for BYOD scenarios?

    A. Azure AD registered devices
    B. Azure AD joined devices

13. Your manager asks that you prevent users from accessing company resources if their personal device is non-compliant. You configure the following device compliance policy in Intune:

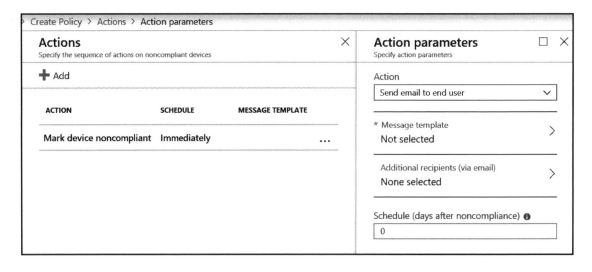

Does this meet the requirement?

A. Yes
B. No

14. You have multiple device compliance policies configured in Intune.
Policy A: Requires a minimum OS of Windows 8.1 for all users.
Policy B: Requires a minimum OS of Windows 10 for members of the Executives group.
Policy C: Requires the encryption of data storage for Seattle users.

Which policy or policies will apply to a Seattle-based member of the Executives group?

A. Policy A and Policy C
B. Policy C
C. Policy B
D. Policy B and Policy C

15. Before your organization can begin using Windows Autopilot to deploy Windows to new devices, what must you configure?

A. A device profile in Intune
B. A deployment profile in Intune
C. An Apple push certificate in Intune
D. Conditional access policies in Intune

16. You need to configure a policy that creates an alert when someone shares a file externally. Where can you do this?

A. **Security & Compliance Center | Alerts**
B. **Security & Compliance Center | Data Loss Prevention**
C. **Security & Compliance Center | Data Governance**
D. **Security & Compliance Center | Threat Management**

17. Review the following retention policy:

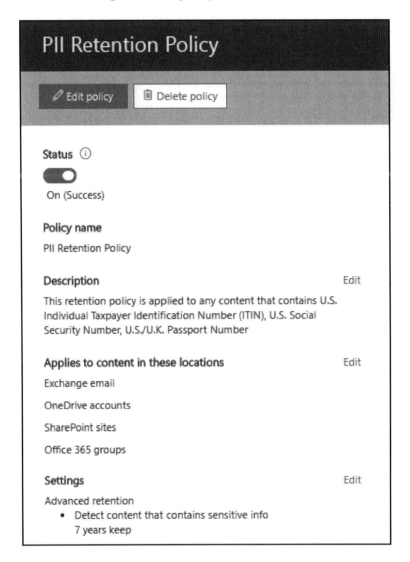

PII Retention Policy

✎ Edit policy   🗑 Delete policy

Status ⓘ

On (Success)

Policy name

PII Retention Policy

Description   Edit

This retention policy is applied to any content that contains U.S. Individual Taxpayer Identification Number (ITIN), U.S. Social Security Number, U.S./U.K. Passport Number

Applies to content in these locations   Edit

Exchange email

OneDrive accounts

SharePoint sites

Office 365 groups

Settings   Edit

Advanced retention
- Detect content that contains sensitive info
  7 years keep

What will happen to a document that contains 10 U.S. Social Security Numbers after 7 years?

    A. Nothing will happen.
    B. It will be deleted.
    C. It will be moved to an archive.
    D. The last owner will be notified.

18. You need to make sure when a user adds documents with sensitivity labels from an Intune-enrolled device to removable media, such as a flash drive, it is encrypted. Then, for example, when that user leaves the company their encryption key would expire and their access to the data, even on the flash drive, would be revoked. Which solution provides this functionality?

    A. BitLocker
    B. Windows Information Protection (WIP)
    C. Data Loss Prevention (DLP)
    D. Azure Identity Protection (AIP)

19. A user deleted a file from their department SharePoint site. Thirteen days later, they emptied their site's recycle bin. For how many more days is the file recoverable from the site collection's (second-stage) recycle bin?

    A. 17 days
    B. 30 days
    C. 80 days
    D. 93 days

20. Complete the following PowerShell to enable auditing of Exchange mailboxes for all users so that activities will begin appearing in the audit log:

```
_____  -ResultSize Unlimited -Filter {RecipientTypeDetails -eq
"UserMailbox"} | _____  -AuditEnabled $true
```

Choose the following two correct portions **in the correct order** to complete the PowerShell line:

    A. `Get-Mailbox`
    B. `Set-Mailbox`
    C. `Get-AuditEnabled`
    D. `Set-AuditEnabled`

15
Mock Exam 2

1. You need to configure Windows Hello for Business as your **Single Sign-On (SSO)** method for 150 on-premise devices joined to Active Directory to access Microsoft 365 services. What must first be in place (select all that apply)?

   A. Devices enrolled in Intune
   B. Devices joined to Azure AD
   C. Devices configured with conditional access policies
   D. Azure Active Directory Connect synchronization

2. Your director asks for a weekly summary of risk events and vulnerabilities with users and identities in Azure AD. What should you do?

   A. Export a report from Compliance Manager.
   B. Add them to the Azure AD Identity Protection weekly digest.
   C. Add them to the risk-level-based alerts in Azure AD Identity Protection.
   D. Pull the Security & Compliance auditing reports.

3. The following sign-in risk policy was created in Azure AD. What will happen when someone signs in and their sign-in is considered high-risk?

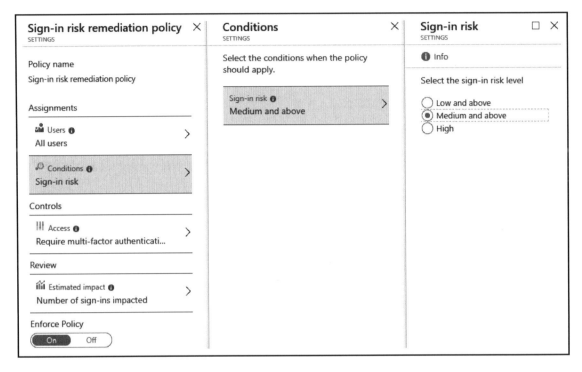

A. They will be blocked from signing in.
B. They will have to sign in using multi-factor authentication.
C. They will be allowed to sign in.

4. You've created a conditional access policy in Azure AD that requires multi-factor authentication when users sign in at a medium or higher sign-in risk level. What can you do to make sure, when users are signing in from an IP address within the Chicago office IP range, that it's not considered a risk and doesn't require MFA?

A. Create a named location in Azure AD.
B. Create an exception to a data loss prevention policy.
C. Create a user risk policy.
D. Modify the sign-in risk policy.

5. You've noticed external users have accessed content on a SharePoint site. You modify the site collection's settings to disallow external sharing. What should you configure to be notified if this policy is changed again?

    A. An audit log alert policy in the Security & Compliance center
    B. A threat management policy in the Security & Compliance center
    C. A compliance policy in the Compliance center
    D. Open an eDiscovery case

6. Your Active Directory domain is named `CompanyA.com` and uses Microsoft System Center Configuration Manager. Your organization manages Windows 8.1 and Windows 10 devices. From the following actions, select the *two* that you need to do in the correct order to analyze the upgrade readiness of the Windows 8.1 devices and the update compliance of the Windows 10 devices.

    A. Add an alias (CNAME) record to the DNS zone of `CompanyA.com`.
    B. Create a Microsoft Azure Log Analytics workspace.
    C. Deploy your commercial ID to all devices.
    D. Configure device compliance in Intune.

7. You need to reduce the likelihood of an anti-phishing impersonation policy generating false positives. You increase the advanced phishing threshold level on the policy. Does this meet the requirement?

    A. Yes
    B. No

8. By following the principle of least privilege, what role should assign someone who needs to be able to review eDiscovery cases they're a member of and perform analysis tasks in Advanced eDiscovery?

    A. Compliance Administrator
    B. eDiscovery Administrator
    C. eDiscovery Manager
    D. Reviewer

9. By following the principle of least privilege, you need to assign someone who needs to be able to read and inspect data protected by Azure Rights Management. You add them to the Security Reader role group in Azure AD. Does this meet the requirement?

    A. Yes
    B. No

10. You are enabling **Azure Information Protection** (**AIP**) for an AD group called Executives. How do you enable it just for the Executives group and not the rest of the organization?

> A. Run the `Add-AadrmRoleBasedAdministrator` cmdlet using AADRM PowerShell.
> B. Create a policy in AIP.
> C. Install the new AIP module by running `Install-Module -Name AIPService`.
> D. Create a label in AIP.

11. Some users in your organization are using Box Business, which they access through MyApps. You want to configure single sign-on for Box through Azure. Where would you do this?

> A. **Azure AD** | **Enterprise applications**
> B. **Azure AD** | **App registrations**
> C. **Azure AD** | **Organizational Relationships**
> D. **Azure AD** | **Application Proxy**

12. The maximum amount of time data is retained in the Microsoft 365 audit log could vary depending on your license. Eventually, E5 licenses and E3 licenses with the Advanced Compliance add-on could retain audit log data for up to a year. Until then, what is the standard audit log retention period for both E3 and E5 licenses?

> A. 30 days
> B. 60 days
> C. 90 days
> D. 180 days

13. You plan to deploy Windows to new devices by using Windows Autopilot. Which three steps are required before you can use Windows Autopilot? Place them in the correct order.

> A. Create device groups.
> B. Create a provisioning package.
> C. Create a device profile.
> D. Create a deployment profile.
> E. Add devices.

14. To integrate **Azure Information Protection (AIP)** with **Cloud App Security (CAS)**, what must you do first to allow monitoring of O365 activity and files from within CAS?

    A. Configure CAS policies.
    B. Set up CAS alerts.
    C. Add O365 as a connected app in CAS.
    D. Upload CAS traffic logs.

15. Your boss asks you to find information about Microsoft's security practices and audit results regarding the protection of your organization's data in O365. Specifically, they need this information to reassure the Compliance department on how Microsoft complies with federal and industry regulations such as appropriate data storage. Where should you look to find this information?

    A. Service Assurance dashboard in the Security & Compliance Center
    B. Azure Information Protection dashboard
    C. Azure Identity Protection dashboard
    D. Alerts dashboard in the Security & Compliance Center

16. You have an alert policy in the Security & Compliance Center that's firing too frequently. What *can't* you do to decrease the frequency of alerts?

    A. Change it from occurrence count-based to anomalous behavior-based.
    B. Increase the policy's activity threshold required before alerting.
    C. Add another condition to the policy to make it more specific, such as narrow it to specific site collections.
    D. Set a daily alert limit.
    E. All options are valid actions to decrease the frequency of alerts.

17. You're configuring a **data loss prevention (DLP)** policy in the Security & Compliance Center. You're including U.S. driver's license numbers as a sensitive data type. When the policy detects 10 or more instances in an email or document, you want to show a policy tip to the user working on the email or document. Where do you configure the policy tip?

    A. **DLP Policy | Choose the information to protect**
    B. **DLP Policy | Choose locations**
    C. **DLP Policy | Policy Settings**
    D. **Microsoft Defender ATP**

18. You're getting a lot of false positives from a DLP policy detecting credit card numbers. What can you do to lessen the likelihood of a DLP policy incorrectly applying to a document?

    A. Increase the confidence level from 75 to 85.
    B. Increase the number of instances required to trigger the policy.
    C. Enable the override option for users to override a policy.
    D. All of the above.

19. What must first be deployed to expand our Azure Information Protection solution to on-premises applications? For example, this deployment would be required to make a **Do Not Forward** button available in Outlook and provide an Information Protection bar in client Office apps. The solution must also support macOS and iOS.

    A. Azure Information Protection (AIP) Client (classic)
    B. Microsoft Defender ATP
    C. Azure Information Protection (AIP) Unified Labelling Client
    D. Azure AD Connect

20. An O365 user in your organization has made a terrible mistake in their OneDrive for Business and they need to restore the entirety of their OneDrive to an earlier point in time. How can you help them do this?

    A. You can't—they'll have to restore whatever they can from the recycle bin and previous versions.
    B. Use PowerShell to restore each item in their OneDrive programmatically to earlier versions.
    C. Use a third-party backup product.
    D. Use Files Restore from the settings (gear) icon in their OneDrive.

Assessments

In this chapter, you can check the answers to the review questions at the end of each chapter, as well as the two mock exams. Each answer includes an explanation and a link to any related documentation. To prepare for the exam, highlight any questions you answered incorrectly and study those topics.

Chapter 1

1. **Answers**: A and B

   Compliance policies can be used to identify devices using operating systems that are too old or new to be compliant. Without a conditional access policy, your options are limited when it comes to responding to noncompliance. Add a conditional access policy to restrict specific access rather than locking a device or just sending an email.

   More information: `https://docs.microsoft.com/en-us/intune/device-compliance-get-started`.

2. **Answer**: C

   Apple devices require a valid MDM push certificate to be configured. If Apple devices are the only devices encountering enrollment issues, that's a good place to start your investigation.

   More information: `https://docs.microsoft.com/en-us/intune/apple-mdm-push-certificate-get`.

Chapter 2

1. **Answer**: B

   Compliance policies alone *can* give you a report listing devices/users that are noncompliant but are not enough to block access. You'll need a conditional access policy as well.

   More information: `https://docs.microsoft.com/en-us/azure/active-directory/conditional-access/conditions#device-state`.

2. **Answer**: D

   Configure named locations in Azure AD so that you can use them with a conditional access policy.

   More information: `https://docs.microsoft.com/en-us/azure/active-directory/conditional-access/location-condition`.

Chapter 3

1. **Answer**: B

   SCCM's dashboard will not include iOS or Android devices; it only supports Windows devices.

   More information: `https://docs.microsoft.com/en-us/sccm/comanage/how-to-monitor#co-management-dashboard`.

2. **Answer**: B

   Retiring a device removes any managed app data and configuration settings, such as Wi-Fi profile settings, and removes the device from the device management dashboard.

   More information: `https://docs.microsoft.com/en-us/intune/devices-wipe#retire`.

Chapter 4

1. **Answer**: B

   By default, the Automated Investigations dashboard shows the last seven days of investigations and categorizes alerts by severity. This would suffice as a solution.

   More information: `https://docs.microsoft.com/en-us/windows/security/` `threat-protection/microsoft-defender-atp/manage-auto-investigation`.

2. **Answer**: C

   In-place upgrades allow you to migrate most data and apps from Windows 7 and 8.1 to Windows 10.

   More information: `https://docs.microsoft.com/en-us/windows/deployment/` `windows-10-deployment-scenarios#in-place-upgrade`.

Chapter 5

1. **Answers**: A and B

   Adding apps to CAS is only part of the process. Typically, you will need to configure some aspects of the app's administration as well. If everything seems okay in CAS, chances are your errors are being authenticated for the app in question or something went awry in your configuration steps. Just check `docs.microsoft.com` and go through their step-by-step instructions for the specific app you're working on to make sure it's been configured and authenticated appropriately.

   More information (specifically on adding G Suite to CAS): `https://docs.` `microsoft.com/en-us/cloud-app-security/connect-google-apps-to-` `microsoft-cloud-app-security`.

2. **Answers:** 1: C, 2: A, 3: B, 4: D (2314)

   You must configure a data source first as you need one to set up the log collector. Once you've done this, you can install Docker on your machine; this will act as the collector. Lastly, you'll configure your firewall and proxy settings to allow the required functionality and verify that everything is working by checking your log collectors in the CAS portal settings.

More information: `https://docs.microsoft.com/en-us/cloud-app-security/` `discovery-docker-windows`.

Chapter 6

1. **Answer:** C

   Nothing will happen to any messages that have been detected as performing domain impersonation. In the policy configuration settings, next to **Action | Domain impersonation**, it states **Don't apply any action**. You can edit the policy or create a new one that will handle it.

   More information: `https://docs.microsoft.com/en-us/office365/` `securitycompliance/set-up-anti-phishing-policies`.

2. **Answer:** B

   ATP Safe Attachments will scan attachments. However, you'll need to configure an **ATP Safe Links** policy to handle it since the document is linked within an email message, as opposed to being directly attached. Within the Safe Links policy configuration, you'll have an option to scan linked documents with Safe Attachments.

   More information: `https://docs.microsoft.com/en-us/office365/` `securitycompliance/set-up-atp-safe-links-policies`.

Chapter 7

1. **Answers:** A, B, C, D

   To restrict access, you'll need to make sure you have devices joined to Azure AD and enrolled in Intune. Then, you need to determine their compliance devices by configuring a device compliance policy in Intune. After that, you have to restrict access for those devices based on their compliance status by creating a conditional access policy in Azure AD.

   More information:
   `https://docs.microsoft.com/en-us/windows/security/threat-protection/mi` `crosoft-defender-atp/configure-conditional-access`.

2. **Answer**: B

The machine's details list the operating system as Windows 10 and its domain as contoso.com, which qualifies it for membership in group 2. Since it has no tags, it will not be in group 1. Since a machine will only be added to the highest-ranking group, group 2 overrules its group 3 eligibility.

More information: https://docs.microsoft.com/en-us/windows/security/ threat-protection/microsoft-defender-atp/machine-groups.

Chapter 8

1. **Answer**: A
Azure AD Identity Protection has sign-in risk policies (to allow MFA requirements) and user risk policies (to allow password resets) that enable automated responses to risky sign-ins. Since the administrator needs the solution to require MFA conditionally, you'd recommend the **Azure AD Identity Protection Sign-in risk policy**.

More information: https://docs.microsoft.com/en-us/azure/active- directory/identity-protection/howto-sign-in-risk-policy.

2. **Answer**: B
From the Security & Compliance Center, you can configure alerts based on user activities, including when someone adds a site collection administrator. Review the table in Chapter 8, *Managing Security Reports and Alerts*, to become more familiar with all the possible alerts you can set up based on activities in Microsoft 365.

More information: https://docs.microsoft.com/en-us/office365/ securitycompliance/create-activity-alerts.

Chapter 9

1. **Answer**: D
DLP policies allow you to stop emails in their tracks when they violate a DLP policy. You can run reports on all policy matches and incidents.

More information: https://docs.microsoft.com/en-us/office365/ securitycompliance/data-loss-prevention-policies.

2. **Answer**: B
   Rule 2 is the most restrictive. DLP policies are applied in terms of the most restrictive first, and if multiple policies are equally restrictive, then they are ordered based on their priority.

   More information: `https://docs.microsoft.com/en-us/office365/securitycompliance/data-loss-prevention-policies`.

Chapter 10

1. **Answer**: D
   AIP policies can be configured to empower end users to protect their own content or adjust any automatically applied protection. This includes the option of requiring justification for adjustments that are made to classification labels.

   More information: `https://docs.microsoft.com/en-us/azure/information-protection/configure-policy`.

2. **Answer**: B
   WIP policies provide you with a number of features, such as managing only company assets on a personal device, remote-wiping company data, and encrypting downloaded data so that, when an employee is terminated, their key is invalid and they can't access content that's been encrypted with it.

   More information: `https://docs.microsoft.com/en-us/windows/security/information-protection/windows-information-protection/overview-create-wip-policy`.

Chapter 11

1. **Answer**: D
   The retention policy is configured so that the content is protected for its lifespan (seven years from creation) and then can *be deleted* after that time period. However, it isn't automatically deleted unless the radio button is changed to **Yes**.

   More information: `https://docs.microsoft.com/en-us/office365/securitycompliance/retention-policies`.

2. **Answer**: C

   Files are only kept for a combined total of 93 days between the site's Recycle bin and the site collection's second-stage Recycle bin. When 94 days have passed, the file will be deleted from both. However, you can contact Microsoft Support for assistance in restoring files in SharePoint Online, *as long as they're within 14 days of their permanent deletion.*

   More information: `https://support.office.com/en-us/article/restore-deleted-items-from-the-site-collection-recycle-bin-5fa924ee-16d7-487b-9a0a-021b9062d14b`.

Chapter 12

1. **Answer**: A

   The O365 Security & Compliance audit log can include SharePoint file activity once enabled. A simple search and export to CSV would be sufficient for this requirement and avoids granting permissions unnecessarily.

   More information: `https://docs.microsoft.com/en-us/office365/securitycompliance/search-the-audit-log-in-security-and-compliance`.

2. **Answer**: D

   If you're only assigning a single role, you can create a new role group in the Exchange admin center and add the **View-Only Audit Logs** role and member(s) that need that ability to search/view the audit logs.

   More information: `https://docs.microsoft.com/en-us/exchange/view-only-audit-logs-role-exchange-2013-help`.

Chapter 13

1. **Answer**: A

   As the question states, the user is not an administrator but should be able to preview results. The role they're missing is **Preview**. This can be assigned by adding them to a new or existing group that has been granted that role.

   More information: `https://docs.microsoft.com/en-us/office365/securitycompliance/assign-ediscovery-permissions`.

2. **Answer**: A

Yes, a guided or new search would accomplish this requirement. You can use either of these (they differ only in user experience) to return content that matches certain criteria, including recipients, keywords, and dates that have been created.

More information: `https://docs.microsoft.com/en-us/office365/securitycompliance/content-search`.

Mock Exam 1

1. **Answers**: F, A, B

`Enable-AadrmSuperUserFeature` enables the Super User Feature and you can add a user with `Add-AadrmSuperUser`. The completed PowerShell code would look like this:

```
Enable-AadrmSuperUserFeature
Add-AadrmSuperUser -EmailAddress "marlon.jackson@contoso.com"
```

More information: `https://docs.microsoft.com/en-us/azure/information-protection/configure-super-users`.

2. **Answer**: A

You cannot move data once Microsoft Defender ATP has been configured. You need to offboard the devices and onboard them again.

More information: `https://docs.microsoft.com/en-us/windows/security/threat-protection/microsoft-defender-atp/data-storage-privacy`.

3. **Answer**: D

Mail flow rules in the Exchange admin center allow you to check email subject lines (and message bodies) for specific words or phrases. Then, you can apply a number of actions, including encryption. With AIP, you can also check for sensitivity labels that have been applied by the sender and configure specific actions for those as well.

More information: `https://docs.microsoft.com/en-us/exchange/security-and-compliance/mail-flow-rules/mail-flow-rule-actions`.

4. **Answer**: B

   The policy specifies a minimum instance count of five SSN occurrences, but the *and* operator between the PII Identifiers and Medical Terms tells us we *also* need something from Medical Terms in order to apply the policy.

   More information: `https://docs.microsoft.com/en-us/office365/securitycompliance/data-loss-prevention-policies`.

5. **Answer**: D

   A sign-in risk policy can automatically respond to specific sign-in risk levels and requires MFA.

   More information: `https://docs.microsoft.com/en-us/azure/active-directory/identity-protection/howto-sign-in-risk-policy`.

6. **Answer**: C

   Exceptions allow you to specify when a policy *shouldn't* apply. In this case, we would configure Company B's domain as an exception when it's a recipient:

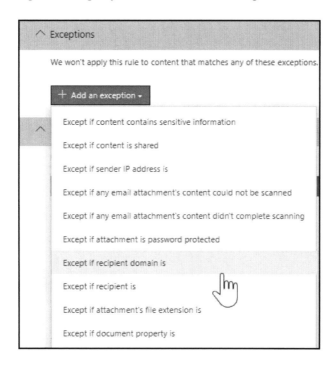

   More information: `https://docs.microsoft.com/en-us/office365/securitycompliance/data-loss-prevention-policies`.

7. **Answer**: C
   The eDiscovery Manager role group in the Security & Compliance Center can have eDiscovery managers and administrators. These roles allow holds to be placed on mailboxes and the management of related cases.

   More information: https://docs.microsoft.com/en-us/office365/securitycompliance/assign-ediscovery-permissions.

8. **Answer**: A
   The policy states that domain impersonation messages will go to **Deleted Items**.

   More information: https://docs.microsoft.com/en-us/office365/securitycompliance/set-up-anti-phishing-policies#set-up-an-anti-phishing-or-atp-anti-phishing-policy.

9. **Answer**: B
   The policy states that user impersonation messages will go to **Quarantine**.

   More information: https://docs.microsoft.com/en-us/office365/securitycompliance/set-up-anti-phishing-policies#set-up-an-anti-phishing-or-atp-anti-phishing-policy.

10. **Answer**: A
    Mailbox intelligence allows you to customize detection of phishing attempts on an individual basis by applying artificial intelligence to learning specific users' typical email behaviors. Configuring mailbox intelligence will allow you to reduce the likelihood of false positives.

    More information: https://docs.microsoft.com/en-us/office365/securitycompliance/set-up-anti-phishing-policies#learn-about-atp-anti-phishing-policy-options.

11. **Answer**: B
    First, you'll need to enable the superuser feature using PowerShell and then assign that role to the user.

    More information: https://docs.microsoft.com/en-us/azure/active-directory/users-groups-roles/directory-assign-admin-roles#security-reader and https://docs.microsoft.com/en-us/azure/information-protection/configure-super-users.

12. **Answer**: A

    Azure AD-registered devices allow individuals to enroll their own personal devices when they choose to sign into Microsoft apps so that they can access work resources. *Joined* devices are work-managed, but these could also be **bring-your-own-devices** (**BYODs**). The self-enrollment route is more common here, but with mobile application management as opposed to mobile device management.

    More information: https://docs.microsoft.com/en-us/azure/active-directory/devices/concept-azure-ad-register.

13. **Answer**: B

    A compliance policy alone isn't enough in this case. You could pair the policy shown here with a conditional access policy to restrict access when a device is marked as non-compliant.

    More information: https://docs.microsoft.com/en-us/intune/conditional-access.

14. **Answer**: D

    The most restrictive policies will take precedence over conflicting policies. In this case, the higher minimum OS requirement will apply.

    More information: https://docs.microsoft.com/en-us/intune/create-compliance-policy.

15. **Answer**: B

    A deployment profile specifies the user groups, deployment mode, end user deployment experience, and other settings pertaining to the deployment of Windows on new devices that are being set up.

    More information: https://docs.microsoft.com/en-us/intune/enrollment-autopilot.

16. **Answer**: A

    Alerts | **Alert policies** is where you can create alert policies to notify specific users of activities and threats in your environment.

    More information: https://docs.microsoft.com/en-us/office365/securitycompliance/alert-policies.

17. **Answer**: A

The policy doesn't specify that it will delete content at the end of the retention period, so it simply *allows* the content to be deleted at that time; however, it does nothing to the file itself. The retention policy protects the file *during* the retention period.

More information: `https://docs.microsoft.com/en-us/office365/securitycompliance/labels`.

18. **Answer**: B

Windows Information Protection (WIP) is available for devices running Windows 10 version 1607 or later. This solution could provide removable media data encryption.

More information: `https://docs.microsoft.com/en-us/windows/security/information-protection/windows-information-protection/protect-enterprise-data-using-wip#why-use-wip`.

19. **Answer**: C

The shared retention period for site recycle bins (the first and second stages) is 93 days. These 93 days could be spent entirely in one or the other (or both, in this case), but movement between the two does not reset or change the retention period. After 93 days from the initial deletion, the file is permanently deleted. In this scenario, the file spent 13 of its 93 days in the first (site) recycle bin and will spend its last 80 days in the second-stage (site collection) recycle bin. If it is deleted early from the second-stage recycle bin (prior to the end of its total 93 days), it is also permanently deleted. Once permanently deleted you can contact Microsoft for assistance in retrieving it within 14 days of permanent deletion before it's unrecoverable even by Microsoft.

More information: `https://docs.microsoft.com/en-us/office365/securitycompliance/office-365-sharepoint-online-data-deletion`.

20. **Answers**: A, B

The following code shows the correct cmdlets to run in order to enable auditing for all Exchange mailboxes:

```
Get-Mailbox -ResultSize Unlimited -Filter {RecipientTypeDetails -eq
"UserMailbox"} | Set-Mailbox -AuditEnabled $true
```

More information: `https://docs.microsoft.com/en-us/Exchange/policy-and-compliance/mailbox-audit-logging/enable-or-disable?view=exchserver-2019#enable-or-disable-mailbox-audit-logging`.

Mock Exam 2

1. **Answers**: A, B, D

   Devices will need to be added to Azure AD and enrolled in Intune before Windows Hello for Business can be configured. Since the devices are joined to Active Directory (on-premise), we'll need Azure AD Connect as well.

   More information: `Chapter 4`, *Planning Windows 10 Deployments*, and `https://docs.microsoft.com/en-us/windows/security/identity-protection/hello-for-business/hello-hybrid-aadj-sso-base`.

2. **Answer**: B

   The weekly digest under **Settings** in Azure AD Identity Protection provides information on users who have been flagged for risk, risk events, and vulnerabilities that have been found; it then emails them a summary each week with links to the relevant dashboards in Azure AD Identity Protection.

   More information: `https://docs.microsoft.com/en-us/azure/active-directory/identity-protection/howto-identity-protection-configure-notifications#weekly-digest-email`.

3. **Answer**: B

   The policy indicates that all users who are signing in at a medium or higher risk need to use multi-factor authentication to sign in.

   More information: `https://docs.microsoft.com/en-us/azure/active-directory/identity-protection/howto-sign-in-risk-policy`.

4. **Answer**: A

   Named locations are IP address ranges that have been labeled as trusted locations. They're used in conditional access policies and to automatically identify false positives in risk detection, as is the case in this question.

   More information: `https://docs.microsoft.com/en-us/azure/active-directory/reports-monitoring/quickstart-configure-named-locations`.

5. **Answer**: A

   The audit log can track information such as changes in sharing policies and many other actions that are taken throughout your organization. Set up an alert policy in the Security & Compliance Center to notify specific people when there has been a change to a sharing policy for specific (or all) sites. The following screenshot shows the **Changed a sharing policy** activity you'd select for this specific alert configuration:

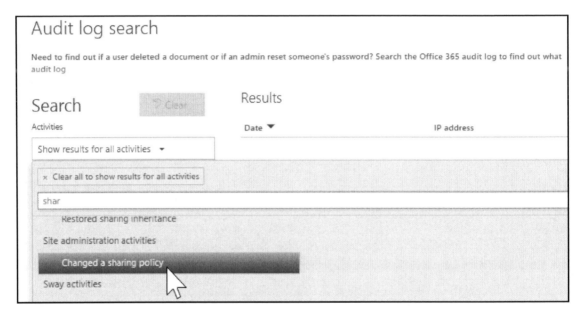

   More information: `https://docs.microsoft.com/en-us/office365/securitycompliance/create-activity-alerts`.

6. **Answers**: B C (in that order)

   Since your organization is managing both Windows 8.1 and Windows 10 devices, you'll need to create a Microsoft Azure Log Analytics workspace and configure all the devices so that they have a commercial ID.

   More information: `https://docs.microsoft.com/en-us/windows/deployment/upgrade/upgrade-readiness-get-started` and `https://docs.microsoft.com/en-us/windows/deployment/update/update-compliance-get-started`.

7. **Answer**: B
   Advanced phishing threshold levels allow you to choose how strict you should be when it comes to flagging messages of varying risk levels. However, you cannot fine-tune these levels to reduce the likelihood of false positives. For this, you'd have to enable mailbox intelligence instead.

   More information: `https://docs.microsoft.com/en-us/office365/securitycompliance/set-up-anti-phishing-policies#learn-about-atp-anti-phishing-policy-options`.

8. **Answer**: D
   The reviewer role is the most restrictive of these options and allows you to view the cases in which the user is a member, and to perform analysis tasks in **Advanced eDiscovery**. This role cannot export search results or create/edit cases or holds.

   More information: `https://docs.microsoft.com/en-us/office365/securitycompliance/assign-ediscovery-permissions#rbac-roles-related-to-ediscovery` and `https://docs.microsoft.com/en-us/office365/securitycompliance/manage-ediscovery-cases#step1_1`.

9. **Answer**: B
   First, you'll need to enable the superuser feature using PowerShell and then assign that role to the user.

   More information: `https://docs.microsoft.com/en-us/azure/active-directory/users-groups-roles/directory-assign-admin-roles#security-reader` and `https://docs.microsoft.com/en-us/azure/information-protection/configure-super-users`.

10. **Answer**: B
    Policies in AIP can only be applied to specific AD groups.

    More information: `https://docs.microsoft.com/en-us/azure/information-protection/configure-policy`.

11. **Answer**: A
    Single Sign-On (SSO) can be configured for many apps, and this can be done from **Azure AD | Enterprise applications**.

    More information: `https://docs.microsoft.com/en-us/azure/active-directory/manage-apps/what-is-application-management` and `https://docs.microsoft.com/en-us/azure/active-directory/saas-apps/box-tutorial`.

12. **Answer**: C

The current standard audit log retention period for both E3 and E5 licenses is 90 days.

More information: https://docs.microsoft.com/en-us/office365/securitycompliance/search-the-audit-log-in-security-and-compliance#frequently-asked-questions.

13. **Answer**: E, A, D

The correct sequence of steps for setting up AutoPilot is adding devices (perhaps by CSV imports), creating device groups, and then creating a deployment profile.

More information: https://docs.microsoft.com/en-us/intune/enrollment-autopilot.

14. **Answer**: C

Before you can start tracking AIP data in CAS, you have to add O365 as a connected app.

More information: https://docs.microsoft.com/en-us/cloud-app-security/connect-office-365-to-microsoft-cloud-app-security.

15. **Answer**: A

The Service Assurance Dashboard is full of documentation that would be helpful in this case. The documentation contains information on Microsoft's security practices and how your data is stored/protected. There are industry-specific documents as well.

More information: https://docs.microsoft.com/en-us/office365/securitycompliance/service-assurance.

16. **Answer**: E

There are many options you can use to decrease the frequency of alerts. This can be configured in the Security & Compliance Center. All of these options could potentially lessen the frequency of alerts.

More information: https://docs.microsoft.com/en-us/office365/securitycompliance/alert-policies#alert-policy-settings.

17. **Answer**: C

The **Policy settings** section in the policy configuration settings, as shown in the following screenshot, provides you with the option to show a policy tip and customize the tip and the email that's sent:

More information: https://docs.microsoft.com/en-us/office365/
securitycompliance/use-notifications-and-policy-tips.

18. **Answer**: D

    All of these options are viable when it comes to reducing the likelihood that a
    DLP policy is improperly applied to a document or email.

    More information: https://docs.microsoft.com/en-us/office365/
    securitycompliance/create-test-tune-dlp-policy#investigate-false-
    positives.

19. **Answer**: C

    The classic **Azure Information Protection (AIP)** client doesn't support macOS
    and iOS and is only used in rare circumstances. The current recommendation
    that *does* support macOS, iOS, and Android is the AIP Unified Labelling client.

    More information: https://docs.microsoft.com/en-us/azure/
    information-protection/rms-client/use-client.

20. **Answer**: D

    Files Restore is available for O365 customers in SharePoint and OneDrive. It
    allows you to restore an entire document library or a user's OneDrive to a
    specific point in time.

    More information: https://support.office.com/en-us/article/restore-your-
    onedrive-fa231298-759d-41cf-bcd0-25ac53eb8a15.

Another Book You May Enjoy

If you enjoyed this book, you may be interested in another book by Packt:

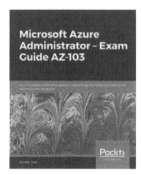

Microsoft Azure Administrator – Exam Guide AZ-103
Sjoukje Zaal

ISBN: 978-1-83882-902-5

- Configure Azure subscription policies and manage resource groups
- Monitor activity log by using Log Analytics
- Modify and deploy Azure Resource Manager (ARM) templates
- Protect your data with Azure Site Recovery
- Learn how to manage identities in Azure
- Monitor and troubleshoot virtual network connectivity
- Manage Azure Active Directory Connect, password sync, and password writeback

Leave a review - let other readers know what you think

Please share your thoughts on this book with others by leaving a review on the site that you bought it from. If you purchased the book from Amazon, please leave us an honest review on this book's Amazon page. This is vital so that other potential readers can see and use your unbiased opinion to make purchasing decisions, we can understand what our customers think about our products, and our authors can see your feedback on the title that they have worked with Packt to create. It will only take a few minutes of your time, but is valuable to other potential customers, our authors, and Packt. Thank you!

Index

Printed in Great Britain
by Amazon